GODZONE

GODZONE

A GUIDE TO THE TRAVELS OF THE SOUL

Michael Riddell

THE PILGRIM PRESS   CLEVELAND

FOR HEMI TE TUTUA

And still you speak.

As I read your hard-won lines

And see the bloody tracks and signs,

I feel your pain . . .

First published in North America 2002
by The Pilgrim Press
700 Prospect Avenue, Cleveland, Ohio 44115-1100 U.S.A.
pilgrimpress.com

ISBN 0-8298-1516-3

Previously published in the United Kingdom
by Lion Publishing Ltd.
Sandy Lane West, Oxford, England
Lion-publishing.co.uk

Printed and bound in the United States of America on acid free paper

07   06   05   04   03   02   5   4   3   2   1

A catalog record for this book is available from the British Library

Library of Congress Cataloging-in-Publication Data

Riddell, Michael.
       Godzone : a guide to the travels of the soul / Michael Riddell.
          p.   cm.
       ISBN 0-8298-1516-3 (pbk. : alk. paper)
       1. God   I. Title: God zone   II. Title.

BT103 .R53   2002
291.4—dc21
                                                      2002029071

CONTENTS

1

Godzone is different. As far as I'm aware, there are no signs indicating where it starts and stops. I have never seen a sign declaring, "You Are Now Entering Godzone." And for good reason. You never do enter it, or leave it for that matter. You're standing in it, as the farmer said to the traveling salesman. Wherever you are, you're in Godzone. It is not a place at all, in the strict sense of the word. In fact, it's a lot easier to say what it isn't than what it is. But even though Godzone isn't anywhere in particular, everywhere is in Godzone—if you see. Perhaps a story will help. Three things are sacred: the journey, the people, and stories. So. Once there was a man who had grown tired and cynical. Nothing brought him wonder or joy, and life itself held no magic. One day he decided to leave his own hometown, where everything was familiar, and search for the perfect Magical City where he had heard that all was different, new, full, and rewarding. So he left. On his journey he found himself in a forest. He settled down for the night, prepared a fire, and had a bite to eat.

Before he retired for the night he was careful to take off his shoes and point them toward his destination. However, unknown to him, while he slept a tramp came during the night and, seeking some fun, turned the shoes around. When the man awoke the next morning he carefully stepped into his shoes and continued on his way to the Magical City. After a few days, he found it—not quite as large as he had imagined. In fact, it looked somewhat familiar. He found a familiar street, knocked on a familiar door, met a familiar family he found there, and lived happily ever after.

Godzone is fairly self-explanatory, You've heard of danger zones and war zones and nuclear-free zones. This is a guide to Godzone. It's the space inhabited by God. Even though you never cross the borders, there is a certain knack to seeing it. It's not immediately obvious. Some people don't believe it exists. Some people don't believe in God. Some people don't see the magic in the universe. Some people think they understand life. These ones will never become travelers (though they will gaze through the windows of their luxury bus aquariums and think they have been somewhere), and so this book is not for them. It is a guide for travelers: for those who feel the constant tug of the road; for people who love life, but love it too much to commit themselves to only one part of it; or for people who stay long enough to learn the truth of a place, but who eventually shoulder their pack and say goodbye. They are on a journey and that is enough. They follow an inner urge, a voice that calls from the depths.

To those, then, who have never quite settled in the world, I offer this guide to Godzone. You are already very close to seeing it. The hunger in you is the longing that comes before the dawn. The half-conscious murmurings, the half-remembered dreams, the half-forgotten insights are all signposts on the way. Let us journey together, then, for this little part of our way. Take off your shoes. You are now entering Godzone.

Visa Requirements

You will be pleased to know that there are no formalities involved in entering Godzone. There are no forms demanding the occupation of your grandmother or the birthplace of your uncle, no long queues while some bloody-minded official examines his fingernails and practices being important, no inquiries as to whether you've got enough money to last you for three months in a luxury hotel. Quite the opposite—the less you have, the easier it is. As that Master Meanderer, Jesus of Nazareth, put it, it's easier to poke a camel through the eye of a needle than for the rich to make it in Godzone—which for anyone who has firsthand experience of trying to poke a camel anywhere, is the same as saying it's hard going.

Jesus walked the dusty paths of Palestine a couple of millennia ago. He also blazed a trail through the Zone, leaving a few signs for those who stumble through the same territory. He wasn't universally popular with religious types, but has always been a friend of wanderers. One of his insights was that you can't really see Godzone unless you get rebirthed. It's not a matter of joining some exclusive club, buying a suit, and becoming Respectable. This would be something like an early death for a traveler and certainly is a long way from what Jesus had in mind. Conformity turns birth into death, which is just about the reverse of what Godzone is all about. What Jesus was saying was that you can't buy your way into Godzone— not with money, nor flattery, nor even good behavior. The only way in is to be rebirthed. Now the person he was talking to at the time was an old man who was Wealthy and Important and Religious. He wanted to enter Godzone all right, but he wasn't too keen on the idea of rebirthing. I guess the thought of having to start all over again was a bit much for him. He laughed at the thought of going back into the womb of his long-dead mother, blessed be she. Too long, too late.

Starting out from scratch in life becomes more attractive the less you have to lose. Important people tend to find the idea repulsive, like having to share a taxi with a mother and three kids. But for people like ourselves with only a pack on our backs, being reborn is just the start of another adventure. In fact, if you've made a few wrong turnings on your journey, having another bash with a clean slate is downright appealing.

So how do you go about rebirthing? Well, the thing about being born is that the baby doesn't actually have much say in the proceedings. There it is, all warm and wet and having a cosmic experience, when suddenly the balloon is punctured and walls start closing in. I dare say if it were to be consulted, the baby would have been quite content to stay where it was. No such luck. It gets pushed out, squeezed through a tunnel clearly too small, and ejected into a bright place full of people waiting to hit it. Rebirthing is something similar. It's not so much something you do as something that's done to you. People who have passed through it can say this and that about it, but if they're honest, they end up having to admit that it's all a bit of a mystery.

What can be said is that you have to want it. Whether out of desperation (the walls start moving in) or longing (you catch sight of something you want on the other side of that tunnel), you have to sign the consent form. There are no illegal entrants to Godzone. They're all there because they wanted to be. Nobody can make anyone do anything they don't want to; adventurers know that from experience. But the illusion is powerful. A lot of people live in prisons they have built for themselves, and curse the bars. In Godzone the wind is called freedom, and it's heady stuff.

The experience of being rebirthed is the kind of thing lots of people achieve, but not everyone wants to talk about. When they do, they describe it in different ways. Words often stagger when they try to carry big experiences. Suffice it to say that when you're born again, all things appear new. It's like you're seeing everything for the first time. New entrants often giggle to themselves. In reality, of course, nothing in the world has changed, except you. The difference is that now you can see. Everything remains as it was, but everything has changed. Perhaps you can understand why people get themselves tangled up when they try to explain all of this to friends.

To see Godzone is to be a part of it. Or, if you prefer, it is only when you are a part of it that you can see it. The first and overwhelming discovery is that God is in it—everywhere. Waving in the trees, laughing in the thunder, shining in old eyes, speaking in the silence. Through it and in it and over it and beyond it—God. This old world of ours is so full of God that you would think it would just burst. The funniest (and saddest) thing in all the world is to hear people arguing about whether God exists or not. Without God, who could argue?

Getting Lost

I guess that all hitchhikers have been lost at some time. It can happen easily enough in a strange place. You only have to fall asleep in some car or other, and then get wakened up to be told you have to get out; this is as far as the ride goes. You finally regain consciousness as the car leaves you in a cloud of dust at the side of the road. You know you're somewhere, but where? Which way have you come to be where you are now? How to know which direction to head in?

Godzoners speak about being lost as the place they all came from. Not lost in a little way, like not knowing what the nearest town is, but lost in a big way. Lost on the face of the world. Waking up one day to find that you don't know how you got to be where you are, and you don't know the way ahead. Lost in the sort of way that a little kid is lost when it can't find its parents; lost so that it hurts. Some react by huddling up into a little ball; others throw themselves into all sorts of things to help them forget; many keep talking in a loud voice to try and impress themselves and others that they know where they're going.

The trendy word for being lost is alienation. Americans have made a multimillion-dollar industry out of it, which keeps psychotherapists off the street. At its most basic level, "lostness" is the feeling of not quite belonging in the world, like somehow you got born in the wrong time or place. It comes on like a bout of car sickness, often when you just thought you had everything together. Being lost is a wound of humanity that everyone carries but nobody shows. Like death, it's kept behind closed doors for fear it should spread.

It is an ache in the deepest part of you, a longing that nothing in the world ever quite touches, a pain that is sometimes haunting and beautiful. From this wound springs all that is great in human art and music, and the most piercing artists and musicians are broken people. The feeling thrives in silence and loneliness, but is easily deadened by the hissing static of "modern" life. People suppress the pain by carefully filling all the gaps in their lives, building sand castles against the sea. When the tide comes in, it sometimes carries them away.

There are many explanations for this "lostness." Often it is termed "depression," and ascribed to a chemical imbalance in the brain. People who suffer from it are sometimes locked away in institutions. However, in essence it is not nearly as complex as it is made out to be. At the risk of pointing out the Emperor's nakedness, may I venture to suggest that the feeling of being lost is an indication that we are lost. This is a radical thought, on a par with the idea that the feeling of hunger indicates a need for food.

We are lost in the sense of the person who suffers from amnesia and wakes in strange surroundings, having forgotten who they are and why they are there. We are lost in the sense of the child separated from its parents, uncertain and frightened of the world. We are lost in the sense of being foreigners in the universe, not knowing the language or the customs, and having no friends. If you don't feel this "lostness," then it is of no value for me or anyone else to try to convince you of it. If you do, it is of no value to try and hide it from yourself.

The awareness of being lost is an indication of grace. It is the beginning of understanding, the disturbing dream that leads to consciousness. Thirst reminds you of your need for drink, "lostness" recalls your need for God. God is the Source and Sustainer of existence, the Rhythm that hums through life, the Lover of the world. Nobody is actually without God, or else they could not live. But many are distant and separated from God in their hearts, and so they suffer the yearning of "lostness."

Some people consider it demeaning to have a "need" for God, or for anything else. They follow the illusion of autonomy. The teaching of the universe is that all things live together. Nothing is totally independent, including God. All that has life is in relationship. This is not a cause for resentment, but for celebration. The tree has need of the soil, the soil has need of the rain, the rain has need of the cloud, the cloud has need of the air, the air has need of the tree, and all have need of God. None detracts from the other, and in their harmony they allow each other to be fully what they are.

Humans are intensely relational creatures. They need each other. They flourish with love and affirmation, shrivel under rejection and loneliness. But the need for relation is never fully satisfied by human companionship, and those who seek it there alone end up sucking each other dry. We have been made to be the children, friends, lovers of God. As an ancient navigator wrote in reflecting on his own journeys, "Our hearts are restless until they find their rest in thee." From God we have proceeded, and it is in harmony with God that we will discover the meaning of who we are.

A story. The village holy man was a person of great spiritual power. When any calamity threatened his people, he would go into a certain part of the forest to meditate. There he would light a fire, say a special prayer, and God would hear him and save the people from disaster. When the time came for him to die, he passed his mantle to a younger sage. He was also wise, but lacked some of the spiritual power of his master. When trouble threatened, he went to the sacred place in the forest and cried out, "Merciful God, forgive me! I do not know how to light the fire, but I am still able to say the prayer." God heard and the miracle was performed.

In the next generation, this man's disciple would go into the forest and say, "I don't know how to light the fire, I have forgotten the prayer, but I know the place and I pray this is enough." It was enough and again salvation was granted. When it fell to the next in the line of village sages to seek God's help, he was distraught. Sitting in his hut, his head in his hands, he spoke in anguish "I am unable to light the fire, and I don't know the prayer, and I cannot even find the place in the forest. All I can do is to tell the story, trusting in God. I only hope it is sufficient." And it was sufficient.

We are the ones who have forgotten even the story of what it means to be human. We have dreamed that we are alone in the universe, and have tried to adjust ourselves to a life of autonomy. In this self-contained isolation, the sense of being lost comes like a fragment of a familiar song. It calls forth an old longing, yet we can't quite remember how the rest of the tune goes. The awareness of being lost is a great gift, the treasure of the poor and the humble. If nurtured carefully, it brings forth the shoots of a life that will never die.

Finding the Way

There is a story of a pilgrim who got lost; a story first told 2000 years ago by a street-wise poet. It concerns a loner who has hit the road to find himself. He wakes up one morning surrounded by half-empty beer bottles with cigarette butts floating in them. He is alone. He vaguely remembers the house full of friends who helped him drink his way through this week's pay packet. It's after ten o'clock in the morning and he realizes that he can kiss his job on the garbage truck goodbye. In a moment of depressing self-realization he sees himself as he really is—lost, lonely, tired.

He finds himself humming Simon and Garfunkel's song "Homeward Bound." Suddenly he thinks to himself, "Why not?" Why not shoulder his pack and head for home, head for the place where his name is known and his face remembered! But what about all those telegrams home for money and the stories he used to milk it? Like how he needed a suit for a job interview, or the time he borrowed the money to do that drug deal and ended up getting ripped off? And he had never even got home for his mother's funeral, having cashed in the return plane ticket a few months earlier. "What the hell," he decided. "I've got nothing to lose. The old man owns a bakery; maybe he'll give me a job on the ovens and I can pay him back over ten years."

So he fronts the road for the last time, and makes his way towards home. Three days later he gets his last ride, which drops him off just short of his destination. As he climbs the hill to the old house, he's a bit apprehensive. He runs over in his mind again the speech he's worked out—a mixture of explanation and apology. He's still playing with the best tone of voice to use when he becomes aware of someone in the distance running and yelling. As he listens, it sounds like his name that's being called. Slowly recognition dawns. The crazy man is his father, running to meet him and screaming out his name.

With a swoop his father is upon him, wrapping his arms around him and crying. The poor boy is dazed, and responds by going into his speech. But his father cuts him off in mid-sentence, holds him with penetrating eyes, and says, "I know." Both crying now, they make their way toward home. Once indoors, his father opens a bottle of his best champagne, takes the steak out of the freezer, and rings around his friends to tell them there's going to be a party tonight. "My son was lost to me," he explains on the phone, "I thought he was dead. But now I've found him and he's come home to stay."

Finding the way is all about coming home. Its heart lies in the discovery that the One you feared to face is not your enemy but your Lover. You find that your return to the Source of Life has been eagerly awaited. Home is the place where you can be yourself, where you are loved and accepted even though your faults are seen. The point about the story of the lost pilgrim is that it wasn't until he made the decision to turn around and head for home that he learned the truth of his father's love.

The thing that keeps most people from the door of Godzone is fear of the sort of reception they're going to get. Partly it's due to the self-appointed PR agents that God has to put up with. They wear ties and shout encouraging things at people, like "God commandeth all men to repent," or "The wages of sin are death." They often carry around old-fashioned pictures of a great judge on a throne or people falling screaming into a pit of fire. It's a bit like Sylvester Stallone doing a promotion for cotton swabs.

But the other part of reluctance to front up to God comes from an inner fear. Nobody knows us like we know ourselves. Wanderers always move on when things get difficult, but on lonely nights they are aware of all the cheap betrayals and tacky motives that cling to the soles of their shoes. There is some deep instinct that makes it plain that to face God means to face yourself, and that's not always an attractive proposition. Especially if the image of God you're carrying round is that of some war-mongering despot sitting on a high throne holding a piece of two by four with which to bash anyone who steps out of line.

To head for home, to begin to find the way back to your place of belonging, takes a lot of courage. You almost have to get to the stage where you give up on life, in order to find it. Sometimes it can feel like dying. It's taking a risk. But then travelers are good at taking risks. The cautious stay at home and die by degrees in front of their television sets. Jesus said that if you guard your life against threat it slips away from you, but if you let go and follow the adventure, you never lose it.

A certain man decided that life was too hard for him to bear. He did not commit suicide. Instead, he bought a large corrugated iron tank, and furnished it simply with a few chosen essentials—a bed to sleep on, books to read, food to eat, an electric light, heating, and even a large crucifix on the wall to remind him of God and help him to pray. There he lived a blameless life without interruption from the world. But there was one great hardship.

Morning and evening, without fail, volleys of bullets would rip through the walls of his tank. He learned to lie on the floor to avoid being shot. Nevertheless, he did at times sustain wounds, and the walls were pierced with many holes that let in the wind and the daylight, and some water when the weather was bad. He plugged up the holes. He cursed the unknown marksman. But the police, when he appealed to them, were unhelpful, and there was little he could do about it on his own.

By degrees he began to use the bullet holes for a positive purpose. He would gaze out through one hole or another and watch the people passing, the children flying kites, the lovers making love, the clouds in the sky, the wind in the trees, and the birds that came to feed on heads of grass. He would forget himself in observing these things.

The day came when the tank rusted and finally fell to pieces. He walked out of it with little regret. There was a man with a gun standing outside.

"I suppose you will kill me now," said the man come out of the tank. "But before you do it, I would like to know one thing. Why have you been persecuting me? Why are you my enemy, when I have never done you any harm?"

The other man laid down the gun and smiled at him. "I am not your enemy," he said. And the man who had come out of the tank saw that there were scars on the other man's hands and feet, and these scars were shining like the sun.

2

INTRODUCTIONS

Godzone is full of God. But who or what is she/he/it? There is no shortage of opinions. For such a small word, "god" gets a lot of mileage. It is used for everything from hand-carved figurines to a stockbroker's last resort. What is God like? Often it seems like asking someone what sex is like—and it depends on their experience as to the sort of answer you get. One of the problems is that God can only be seen properly from within Godzone. Anyone can use the word; not everyone has experienced the reality.

This shouldn't unduly faze an adventurer. You are used to meeting people on the road and weighing up the stories they tell you. You judge them by what you've learned from the road, and the way the storyteller comes across. You learn never to trust people with a glossy pamphlet in their hand, or shiny shoes on their feet, nor to believe a person who has only traveled in their head. You listen to them all, of course. But when it comes down to your own journey, you want to be sure about the path you follow.

Concerning God, listen only to those who have been into the heartland of Godzone. Trust only travelers who have known the reality for themselves. You have learned wisdom from your own travels; don't discard it lightly. There are many self-styled hawkers of divinity. They peddle salvation like snake oil, make truth into a product to be sold. Enjoy them for their entertainment value, but their stories are no more to be relied upon than cotton candy can fix malnutrition.

The best way to get to know someone is to spend a bit of time with them. Two days together on the road between Fès and Marrakech reveals a lot. And so with God. You can never learn enough about God to satisfy the hunger of your soul. Only getting to know God is sufficient for that. In Hebrew the word "to know" is the same as that for sexual union. It gives new meaning to "getting to know" somebody. It's knowledge in depth, a knowing that involves body, mind, and spirit, a knowing that moves you. This is the only sort of knowledge that's valid when it comes to God.

Getting to know God is a cosmic experience, and not just for nostalgic hippies. It's a strange feeling to meet Someone who has always known you. But it's no good trying to describe it; you have to have been there. So let me perform a few introductions. God already knows you, from about as far back as it's possible to go. You sort of know God, too, but sometimes you've forgotten the name. Worse, sometimes you've filled the name with your own meanings. Let me reintroduce you, with a small prayer that it might lead to something more.

Identikit Pictures

And a small explanation. It is well said that no one can see God and live. This is not because anyone is going to punish you for prying. You are expected to poke and prod and lift the covers. But the plain fact of it is that none of us can handle a face-on session with the Source of all that is. Mere mortals kind of get blown away by the intensity of God. To see God is to be consumed by God, and that's not to be this side of the river. So, like watching an eclipse of the sun, we have to have God filtered a little.

God casts a lot of shadows in the world. By listening to many voices and putting together the pieces of truth, you can come up with a sort of identikit picture of God. It's good, because it gives you an idea of what you're looking for. But like a postcard of a Monet, it's not the same as the real thing. God shows up best in people, and one of the things you learn in Godzone is to see the bits of God in everyone.

Some very special people show a lot of God to the world. They are gifts to us in many different times and cultures. Jesus is unique in being so full of God as to become transparent. When people looked at him they saw clear through to God—filtered a little so that it didn't scorch the retinas, but God nonetheless. The God I want to introduce to you is the God seen in Jesus of Nazareth.

That is not to say you can't see God in others. There is the story of the three blind men who went in search of an elephant. They traveled together and eventually located the mythical beast. The elephant tolerated the indignity of their explorations, as they used their hands to examine it. They shortly drew aside to share their new wisdom.

"An elephant is round and solid, like the trunk of a great tree," said the one who had clung to a leg.

"Not so," argued the second who had grasped the tail. "Rather, the elephant is thin and springy, like a sapling that bends in the breeze. And though it reaches up into the heavens, at its nether end it has a bush like an Arab's beard."

"May the pox of a thousand chickens ream your inner passages for telling such a lie," said the third who had encountered the trunk. "The elephant is a strong and supple tunnel with the breath of life within it. It reaches out into every corner to seek what it might find."

The story ends just in time, before the three blind men are able to make doctrines of their differing experiences, and begin a holy war. The elephant retreated sadly into the jungle.

None of us holds the exclusive understanding of God. But you can't look in three directions at once. If your focus is to be good, your gaze must be single. God is beyond our visions, and not to be contained by them. However, the truth of God can be known by us all, and I have found in Jesus a guide and pioneer to lead me to the beating heart of God. So allow me to continue with the introduction.

Lover

The word that defines God, that carries through when all the others have stumbled and fallen, is love. Love is God's essence, and prefaces everything else that can be said. God is love.

The word itself is, of course, sloppy. The Mindbenders have used it to sell chocolate and perfume. Teenagers are convinced that the rush of hormones flooding their budding bodies is love. Pulp novelists produce swamps of emotional slush that they casually describe as love stories. Politicians appeal to love of country when the war economy is at a low ebb. Lonely people use each other's bodies, faking love by making love. Love has been emptied of meaning, trivialized like Bach played on a kazoo.

Nevertheless, genuine love exists. Those who have been ravaged by it find it disappointing to be left with no other word to use for the storm in their spirit. It is perhaps easier to take hate and reverse it than to allow the flaccidity of "love" to continue to mislead. However, we are left with it. God *is* love. Love in its uncut form is to be found in God. The river of love between two people is at its deepest point an intimation of the heart of God. But it is still only an intimation, the snatch of a sax solo carried on the night.

Love without loving is as frustrating as a destination without a ride. God is not only love, but Lover. That is to say that the heart of God has gone out from itself to envelop the universe. Love is the source of its existence, love the energy streaming through it, love the end toward which it moves. The love of God is not static; it is not the pot at the end of the rainbow. It is moving, acting, piercing, wooing, fondling, creating.

God is your Lover, the One who danced with joy at your birth, who dreamed you into being in the first place; the One who has tracked you down the back streets of your life, whispering to you in the night, calling to you from the darkness. God is not so remote as to be only *the* Lover. God is *your* Lover: the One who knows you by name.

You are on the move. You change city, country, friends, and songs, sometimes even socks. But there is one traveling companion that never changes, who has been with you from the beginning and will be there when you catch your last ride. God sticks closer than a lonely dog and, though discouraged from tagging along, is every bit as difficult to shake off.

This is, naturally, terrifying. We flee from our Lover like hippies from hard labor. We disguise ourselves, wear masks to hide behind. We invent images of God that can be easily dismissed, as if burning a plastic Beatles wig could diminish the music. In some deep part of us we know that to open ourselves to this Love is to be transformed once and for all. Perhaps that is why we became wanderers in the first place. Not, as we like to think, that we are searching, but running.

Our Lover is more persistent than Butch Cassidy's posse. God haunts our dreams, sighs in the wind, shines in the eyes of a friend, calls in the cry of a bird. It is a Love that will not let us go, that never gives up hope of our hearing, seeing, receiving. And God has the patience of a donkey on tranquilizers. God will wait for you. Follow you through the valleys and swamps, the bitterness and heartache, the betrayals and loneliness. When you have given up on everyone else and everyone else has given up on you, your Lover will be there, waiting.

God is a seducer, not a rapist. Your freedom will be safer than Snow White's innocence. Love is not to be imposed. That is why God waits, for your response. But you will be wooed. You need to be aware that the hearts of some very cynical people have been won. Hardened travelers have found the crust of their hearts gently dissolved. Some who have thrown themselves off the edge of the world in a desperate bid for destruction have wakened to find themselves in the arms of God. Resisting God is only slightly more difficult than determining than value of pi, and you have to hold out longer.

Jacob was a desert traveler; a nomad, a hitchhiker before his time. Under the stars he met a stranger, a dark man with eyes that glistened. Jacob greeted the man, sizing him up. He recognized a fellow sojourner, a desert dweller. He challenged him to a wrestling match. Jacob liked a challenge, liked to pit himself against the unknown. They set to in the sandy wastes. The stranger was the equal of Jacob. At times it seemed that he was getting the better of the fight, but Jacob was not about to surrender. He had survived thus far on his strength and his wits and had come through when all had seemed lost.

The two wrestled right through the night. It was at first light, when the sky ached with color, that Jacob finally got the advantage. He had the stranger pinned, held him captive. Quietly the stranger put out his hand and touched Jacob on the thigh, and his hip was thrown immediately and painfully out of joint. In that moment, Jacob recognized the Stranger. He had been struggling against his Lover. Being an opportunist, Jacob demanded a blessing from the Stranger. His gift was a new name, Israel, which means "the one who strives with God." In overcoming God you are overcome. God enjoys a good fight as much as an Irish publican. From hearts that struggle there is the hope of honest love. A lover does not want gratitude or compliance; soggy affection is no more appealing than cold porridge. Nothing short of a free and equal passion will suffice. If such love must be won from long and painful wrestling, better that than an insipid pretense that does not stir the gut. It is possible to keep running for a long time. But once you join battle with the Stranger, you are at risk.

Love, of course, needs a sign. How are you to know that the silent stranger is not your enemy, enticing you with a delicate web, which will later serve as a spider's placemat? If you are to believe that God is your Lover, it will take more than a tout's testimony. The evidence is there for those who are looking. It is present in the universe itself, in the deep hum of creation. There is the recognition of your heart, which knows more than you give it credit for. There are the people who have been loved, and themselves become lovers.

There is the sign of Jesus, who, when washed clean of religious mire, becomes a love poem from God to us. Jesus was obsessed by God, full of God. His life burned briefly as a beacon to light the way. He not only talked about but embodied the love that is God. He made our Lover present and believable to the poor and the broken. When the world could stand his love no longer, and hammered it to a cross, he still would not stop loving. He died with a prayer on his lips for those who cursed him. It is not surprising that a love so strong could not be extinguished by death.

The final sign is your own experience. You cannot expect to know what love is by reading about it in a book. You must take the risk of opening yourself to it. You must join the struggle with your Lover. Only then will you know for a certainty.

Sufferer

To love is to suffer. When you open your heart to another, you risk pain as a diver risks the bends. You give of yourself, and the one you love carries that part which you have given. If the lover betrays your love, you can no more withdraw it than you can cash a canceled check. You can only endure the pain and grow through it. Some people who have their heart torn resolve never to open it again, never to take the risk of leaving the door open to further pain. But the love and the pain go together, and few of us can live without love for any length of time. Some travelers have relationships in which they exchange only bodies and minds. But the road-wise know that you get what you give, and that holding back on love is as foolish as ignoring your bladder. Better to take the love with the suffering than to miss out on both.

A dog with a bone in its mouth came to a still pool. As it looked into the water it saw its own reflection. The dog growled; the reflection growled back. The other dog's bone looked better. Finally the dog opened its mouth to make a grab for the juicier bone, and was astonished by a splash and an empty mouth.

The greater the love, the greater the suffering. God, the original Lover, is also the original Sufferer. All the pain of the universe floods into that great heart. God invented passion, which is both the abandon of love and the agony of suffering. To know one is to know the other; to have a capacity for love is to have an equal capacity for pain. The Doctors of Doctrine, the Rulemakers and Scorekeepers, would have us believe that God cannot suffer. Through this cruel canon, they deny the love of God. They create a god in their own image, a thin loveless boring parody of a god. Unfortunately this anemic deity has found its place in much dutiful religion.

An even darker thought comes from the moralists and inquisitors—that God causes suffering. They paint a picture of a sadistic tyrant god, who rules through fear and threat of punishment. Such a demon god it would be our duty to resist with all our strength. We can do without a sarcastic schoolteacher of the sky. But why should we listen to the nonsense of those who seek to bolster their own inadequacy through flaunting a divine despot?

It will not take long for some gray-faced cynic to ask why, then, should God allow suffering to exist in the universe. If God is love, why should anyone suffer? Why doesn't the

Cosmic Plumber "fix" things once and for all? This is a real question, and drives right to the heart of faith. However, suffering is not an algebra problem to be solved. It is an agony to be born. Like a bloody birth, suffering springs from letting be.

True love can only exist between free beings. Try buying it or demanding it—it disappears faster than a bouncer's sense of humor. So when the Lover sung the universe into existence, freedom was woven into its music, freedom to accept or reject the Composer of the symphony, freedom to accept or reject the unique score that belongs to each organism of life, freedom for harmony or discord, for good or evil.

There is no explanation for suffering, only understanding; no solution, only participation. Elie Wiesel tells a story out of the furnace of Auschwitz.

The SS seemed more preoccupied, more disturbed than usual. To hang a young boy in front of thousands of spectators was no light matter. The head of the camp read the verdict. All eyes were on the child. He was lividly pale, almost calm, biting his lips. The gallows threw its shadow over him . . . The three victims mounted together onto chairs. The three necks were placed at the same moment within the nooses. "Long live liberty!" cried the two adults. But the child was silent.

"Where is God! Where is he?" someone behind me asked. At a sign from the head of the camp, the three chairs tipped over. Total silence throughout the camp. On the horizon the sun was setting. "Bare your heads!" yelled the head of the camp. His voice was raucous. We were weeping. "Cover your heads!" Then the march past began. The two adults were no longer alive. Their tongues hung swollen, blue-tinged. But the third rope was still moving; being so light, the child was still alive.

For more than half an hour he stayed there, struggling between life and death, dying in slow agony under our eyes. And we had to look at him full in the face. He was still alive when I passed in front of him. His tongue was still red, his eyes not yet glazed. Behind me, I heard the same man asking: "Where is God now?" And I heard a voice within me answer him: "Where is he? Here he is—hanging on the gallows . . ."

God suffers with us. God shares in the agony of a scarred humanity. Like a mother watching her druggie son dissolve before her eyes, torn with the memory of his babyhood, taunted by the hopes she once held for him, God watches and hurts. Beyond interference, beyond control, helpless before a gut-wrenching love, waiting and keening. A mother has no escape from the tragedy of her children; she is condemned to be crushed beneath the juggernaut of devotion.

So with God who aches for you and through you. God is the God of the cross, who will love you though you pierce his hands with nails. God will take what you dish out. Holocaust or harpoon, My Lai or mockery. The love of God is suffering love, a love that has won over its bitterest enemies. A love that has waited all this time, for you.

Dreamer

Living things are characterized by movement. They grow and change, pulse and vibrate. Dead things do not move. They are static, unchanging, flat as a cat on the tarmac. Travelers resist death by instinct. They are sure at some deep level of consciousness that there is a state of living death, and that if you stand still too long, you might catch it. This much they have in common with God. God is never still. God has been on the way somewhere since before time was dreamed of. God is a Mover and Trailblazer, a Dancer and Groundbreaker.

God is alive! The universe testifies to it. Novas explode, amoebas wriggle, winds stir, oceans heave, gazelles leap, ants scurry. Only leather-shod Taxidermists who no longer allow their bare feet to touch the earth could have sewn together a static god. If God is in any danger of death, it is from the

Technocrats and Numbercrunchers who form the new priesthood of the world. They have reduced beauty to anatomy, death to physiology, the moon to a landing site. They are so busy analyzing that they forget to see.

Occasionally, even the most analytical of scientists neglects scrutiny and is overwhelmed by life. Watching beavers and otters play can become a moment of insight.

"I was transfixed. As I now recall it, there was only one sensation in my head, pure elation mixed with amazement at such perfection. Swept off my feet, I floated from one side to the other, swiveling my brain, staring astounded at the beavers, then at the otters . . . I wished for no news about the physiology of their breathing, the coordination of their muscles, their vision, their endocrine systems, their digestive tracts . . . All I asked for was the full hairy complexity, then in front of my eyes, of whole, intact beavers and otters in motion."

It was God who dreamed up the "full hairy complexity" of beavers and otters—not in a laboratory, nor with a set of plans and a projected budget. It is possible to have knowledge without understanding, to strain out facts and leave behind truth. We airheads who walk may have no degrees or white coats, but we know for certain that the world is not made of laws and Lego. The universe consists of love and energy and freedom and movement—and God.

Everything alive is moving, even that which appears to stand still. Call it evolution if you will. Call it creation if you prefer. The engine that drives the universe forward is not natural selection but the dreaming of God. God's dreams invade the world as a song haunts your mind; summoning, luring, calling. Where they find resonance in an answering heart (and even the mountains have hearts), there is movement, newness. Imagination in all its forms is the antenna of the spirit; dreaming is the language. God calls the tune; some of us dance. This waltz between God and the world is the source of all that is, and more importantly, what is yet to be.

A young boy came to watch a sculptor at work. In a hall with a high ceiling stood a massive block of stone, surrounded by canvas sheets. The sculptor walked round and round the block before setting to with a hammer and chisel. Some months later the small boy returned. The block of stone had disappeared, and in its place stood a magnificent lion, crouched and ready to spring. It was so real that the boy was nervous to touch it, then relieved to find the coolness of granite beneath his fingers. The lion was truly wonderful. But the boy was puzzled. "Mister," he said to the sculptor, "How did you know that lion was in the rock?"

"I knew the lion was in the rock," replied the artist, "because I saw it first in my heart."

It is good news to nomads to learn that God is a Mover and a Dreamer. Our journeys have often been inspired by dreams. We know their unsettling power, how they lead us on to new and undiscovered horizons. God is the Primeval Hitchhiker; recognizing the beauty of all that has been and is, but never quite being able to cure the itch for something new and different. God has never "settled down." God does not own a television set, nor play bowls. God does read poetry, and rage.

The long and winding road that we cannot stop following is one that has been traveled before. Up ahead of us somewhere God is still trying to work out which way it goes.

Healer

Healing means to be made whole. It assumes that something or someone has fallen apart. As freedom follows the discovery of chains, healing depends on a recognition that something is wrong. The basic problem with the universe, and with people, is one of disintegration, of separation. It is a separation between God, the Source of Life, and the rest of creation. This falling apart shows itself in many different forms: in disease, in war, in incest, in cruelty, in starvation.

God is leading us out of chaos and toward wholeness. God is Healer of our brokenness. But as the doctor said to the patient with foreign currency, health involves change. The first stage of this is awareness. Jesus said that those who are well have no need of a healer. He well knew that the Beautiful People with even teeth are often the least whole. But he also knew that until they recognized their brokenness, there could be no healing. That's one reason why Jesus spent his time with "sinners"; they knew their own inner chaos.

There are two ways of healing. One is that of treating the symptoms. This is the focus of medicine in the West, one that gets a giggle in Beijing. It is not without value but does not go deep enough to bring lasting change. Auschwitz requires more than sticking plaster, or even remorse. Hiroshima is cured not through arms negotiations, but by surgery to make hearts open. Unfortunately the hunger of our age is for "fixing." Never mind death, so long as the corpse looks beautiful.

Jesus once came across ten lepers as he was on the road between Samaria and Galilee. They cried out to him. They wanted to be healed. Or so they said. What they really wanted was to be rid of the leprosy. This is not quite the same thing. Jesus responded to them on the level they asked. They were cleansed of their leprosy. Later one of them returned to thank Jesus, full of the joy of God. Jesus, noting that the man was alone, remarked astutely that while ten lepers had been cured, only one had been healed.

Wholeness does not exist in the absence of a relationship with God, any more than babies can be made single-handedly. The sickness that has infected existence is fragmentation. When life tears loose from its center, it comes apart. When the center is restored, wholeness begins. This is the second type of healing, and the only true healing. Its basis is reconciliation —the joining together of that which has fallen apart.

When you fall out with someone you want to avoid them. You may have shared the back seat of a VW with them for two hundred miles, but after a row, you separate. If you meet your former friend in a cafe in the next town, you ignore them. You especially avoid the meeting of eyes, because you can't stand either the pain of separation or the tug of friendship mixed with it. Those of us who have fallen out with God likewise feel bad about it. We try to hide, though that's difficult when the one looking for you is God.

That's what God is up to—looking for you. The separation is one-sided, because God loves enough to understand everything that has happened. God just wants you back. But it's difficult getting close enough to let you know. The search for some way of getting it across goes on. Jesus was a love letter from God. It read "Come on home—we're waiting for you. There's nothing you have done or can do that will make me stop loving you. I'll even die for you if that's what it takes." It made people feel guilty so they nailed it to the cross. Healing involves you getting the message and believing it.

There once was a very holy man called Abraham. He was a great ascetic. He had eaten nothing but herbs and roots for fifty years. He lived simply and very austerely in total self-discipline. One day his brother died and left a niece, and there was no one to care for her. So Abraham took her in and nourished and cherished her. Her name was Mary, and she grew up to be beautiful both in body and in spirit. She followed Abraham, prayed with him, and was filled with grace.

One day a wandering monk came to hear a word from Abraham and was smitten by the beauty of his niece. While taking advantage of the hospitality offered by Abraham, who was out visiting other monks, he was overcome by lust and raped her. She was so mortified and ashamed that she stayed away from Abraham and in fact fled to the city where, feeling so violated and disgraced, she became a prostitute.

Abraham searched for her. He scoured the hills, sent out messengers, and posted notices around the local villages. But all in vain, until he heard one day some years later that Mary was plying her trade at a certain tavern. Abraham disguised himself as a military man with all the regalia, went to the tavern, and ordered bottles of wine and rich meat. Though he had not eaten meat for fifty years, that night he ate and drank to his heart's content. After he finished his dinner, he asked the keeper for the "wench" named Mary: "I have come a long way for the love of Mary."

She was brought to him, and she did not recognize this hard-eating, hard-drinking soldier. He grabbed her and she said coquettishly, "What do you want?" And he looked into her eyes and said, "I have come a long way for the love of Mary." She recognized her uncle and wept bitterly for the sorrow of their separation, and then she returned home with him.

God has traveled to hell and back for the love of the universe. Our healing awaits only our return. When the center is replaced, the broken bits begin to come back into order. A note of caution. To be healed does not mean to be fixed. It is not only possible, but likely, for a paraplegic who is healed to remain in a wheelchair. A schizophrenic who has entered Godzone may still need to take medication. God chooses such to be the most disarming agents of Godzone. Through their brokenness they have journeyed to the center and received the key to open a thousand doors—acceptance.

To be healed is to come back into relationship with God the Healer. It is to enter Godzone. Godzone is defined by relationship with God. Where God's love is returned, there is Godzone. That is why it is everywhere and nowhere. It is your home, your place of belonging. God is the Stranger you have always known, Godzone the house of your secret longing. Let us explore it together.

3

THE LIE OF THE LAND

People on the road get good at finding their way around. When you've only got two days in a town, you learn to navigate by instinct. You also get to be good at figuring when the car you hitched a ride in has just turned off the road you wanted to follow. The trick is to get a feel for the country you're in, where the sun rises and sets, where the wind comes from, which side the sea is on in relation to the mountains. You need to know the lie of the land.

Godzone has a geography too, though it's a little different from any you've ever seen before. If you want to find your way around, it's helpful to know something of the terrain. There are no borders, but there is a center. All roads in Godzone lead to the center, and the full-time occupation of travelers is getting further along the road they're on. Journeying doesn't stop when you enter Godzone. In some ways it begins in earnest. The one constant is the road. It keeps on stretching out in front of you. Sometimes it fades so you can barely trace it. When shadows fall across it, the journey gets cold and scary. Further on it passes by a river on a sunny day, and you shiver with delight as you do a bit of skinny dipping. The road holds all these experiences together and makes of them one journey. Even when the road is hard, it is still leading somewhere. As all veterans of snakes and ladders know, players must follow their own paths. You don't always travel alone, and some of the best parts are with companions, but nobody else follows exactly the same route as you. The features of the land can be shared from experience, but no one can slog your path for you. The following are simply landmarks for you to get your bearings by. May the road rise up to meet you!

Peaks

The higher you get, the clearer the air becomes. In the mountains it is cold and spiced. To climb to the top of a mountain gives not only a sense of accomplishment, but a chance to pause and rest. If it's a Swiss mountain you can have a coffee in the restaurant. From your perch on the top of the world you see the lie of the land. You can trace the way you have come and look down on the towns and villages so small below. And you can see what had previously been hidden—the other side of the mountain. At the top of a peak is a good place to think about where you have come from and where you are going to. The peaks of Godzone are dazzling. Beside them the Matterhorn is misshapen, Everest stunted. They are the places where the mists fall away and everything becomes clear. You wonder how you could ever have been so dumb as to doubt or stumble, when it is all so obvious. You see the road stretching out ahead of you, heading deep into the center. If the peak is especially high, you may see near the edge of the horizon a great river, and beyond it a strange light. The land that unfurls before your eyes is rich and mysterious. It draws you like a cold beer on a hot day.

Some mountains stand out from the crowd. The better known peaks of Godzone have names. Many roads lead to them, and like a pay phone that allows free toll calls, their whereabouts are known by travelers near and far. They are renowned as vantage points from which the journey comes into perspective. Some of them you may already have scaled without realizing that they were a part of Godzone. Check these ones.

Joy

Joy is not the same as happiness. Happiness depends on what happens. Happiness is a Porsche with a stereo stopping for you when it just started raining. Joy may rise in the midst of a thunderstorm with not a car to be seen. Happiness is finding a wallet full of twenty-dollar notes with no identification in it. Joy could hit you as you give your last five dollars to a lovable rogue with an unlikely story. Happiness is the preserve of the lucky, the wealthy, and the successful. Joy belongs to any who find it, and the poor seem to find more of it than most.

Sometimes if you twang a note on a guitar, you can make a string on a different guitar vibrate. It's called resonance. Joy is when your heart picks up the vibrations of God and, for a brief period of time, beats in harmony; when your love echoes God's love; when your gift resonates with God's. There are moments when you see the funny side of life through God's eyes, and then you just laugh and laugh and laugh. People think you're crazy, because there's no obvious reason to be cracking up; it's just that you've seen the cosmic joke once more.

At other times it's just a deep warm glow; a long slow lingering orgasm of well-being. It floods up through you like a warm delicious flush. It makes your eyes shine. In fact you can pick people in a state of joy, because even if they are crippled with arthritis, their eyes glisten like jewels. Joy is a state of intense aliveness. The more your heart melds with God's, the more often joy erupts. The more joy, the higher you get, and the further you can see into the distance. Joyful people are good guides to the heartland.

But joy can be elusive. The more you seek it, the more it flees away. Joy cannot be bought or sold, and will not be preserved. Those who chase it for the buzz of it find themselves with sore face muscles from trying to fake it. A devoted eighty-year-old couple may find more joy in cutting each other's toenails than two young sexual athletes squeeze out of a whole night of frantic position-changing. You grasp for it and it is gone. You open your hand to feel the rain and your heart leaps. Joy is like a homing beacon—it keeps you on track. If you lose it, you know you've wandered off the path somewhere. It's not a constant hum—more like an intermittent beep to let you know you're doing okay. Joy is the sort of harmonic that is produced by tuning your life to your Lover. When it rings in your ear, you know the music can start again. The melody strummed from a life in tune would break the heart of Hitler.

Relinquishment

Once upon a time there was an old man from the lovely island of Crete. He loved his land with a deep and beautiful intensity, so much so that when he knew that he was about to die he had his sons bring him outside and lay him on his beloved earth. As he was about to expire he reached down by his side and clutched some earth into his hands. He died a happy man. He then appeared before heaven's gates. God, as an old white-bearded man, came out to greet him.

"Welcome," he said. "You've been a good man. Please, come into the joys of heaven."

But as the old man started to enter the pearly gates, God said, "Please. You must let the soil go."

"Never!" said the old man, stepping back. "Never!"

And so God departed sadly, leaving the old man outside the gates.

A few eons went by. God came out again, this time as a friend, an old drinking crony. They had a few drinks, told some stories, and then God said, "All right, now it's time to enter heaven, friend. Let's go." And they started for the pearly gates. And once more God requested that the old man let go of this soil and once more he refused. More eons rolled by. God came out once more, this time as a delightful and playful granddaughter.

"Oh Grandad," she said, "You're so wonderful and we all miss you. Please come inside with me."

The old man nodded and she helped him up, for by this time he had grown very old and arthritic—in fact, so arthritic was he that he had to prop up the right hand holding Crete's soil with his left hand. They moved toward the pearly gates, and at this point his strength quite gave out. His gnarled fingers would no longer stay clenched in a fist, with the result that the soil sifted out between them until his hand was empty. He then entered heaven, and the first thing he saw was his beloved island.

The more you carry on your back, the harder you find it to move. Fresh-faced beginners on the road have large clean packs, containing such vital necessities as traveling irons. The further they travel, the more they find they are able to do without. Possessions weigh people down. Nobody climbs a mountain pulling a trailer behind them. To move on and up in Godzone, you have to learn to let go. This can be a very painful process, sometimes seeming like death itself. To grasp, to cling, to hold on, these come naturally. To let go without being forced to is to share in the life of God.

Relinquishment leads to the heights where the air is pure. It clears through the complexity of life as a sharp ax splits dry wood. Possessions, be they things or ideas, cloud the vision. They clutter the spirit and deaden the voice of God. The only way to regain your senses, to see and hear again, is to become empty. This is not a matter of taking yourself off to a hermit's cave. It simply means to open the hands, to have but not to hold, to enjoy but not to possess.

As a much-traveled explorer of the heartland once said, you learn this not out of a book, but by tramping forty kilometers with sore feet in the rain. Letting go is not a lesson that is learned once for all. It is like peeling the layers off an onion, each time getting closer and closer to the heart. To choose to be poor is to become available to God. Many people spend their lives acquiring and possessing. The pilgrims of Godzone pursue life through giving and letting go.

A certain woman had a vivid dream. In it she saw a man with untidy long hair and bare feet sitting on a bench outside the post office. A voice said to her that if she were to ask this man, he would give her something which would make her rich forever. She woke and shrugged the dream off. But the next day while walking through town, she saw the man from her dream sitting on the bench outside the post office. Feeling somewhat foolish, she approached the man and explained her dream. He listened, and then reached into his rucksack. He produced an enormous gold nugget, saying, "I found this beside the road. Here, it's yours if you want it." She looked longingly at the nugget. It was huge, sufficient to make her wealthy. That night she could not sleep, tossing and turning in her bed. At dawn she set off to find the tramp, who was sleeping under a tree in the park. She woke him and said, "Give me that wealth that makes it possible for you to give this treasure away."

Celebration

Jesus was one who learned to let go of everything, including life itself. And yet he gained a reputation amongst the Misery Merchants as a glutton and a drunkard. Their grim-faced god did not allow unseemly outbreaks of fun. God, on the other hand, loves to party. Any excuse will do to transform the mundane into a special occasion. Godzoners are a people who live by celebration as a fire lives by burning.

It is the fallacy of the facile to believe that celebration is expensive. Socialites select their wines, fly in delicacies, and hire orchestras in a hunger to impress. But any hitchhiker knows that two tin cans and half a bottle of Stones Green Ginger Wine is grounds enough for a good time. To light a fire on the beach at night, to sing protest songs out of key, to laugh or cry together over a packet of fish and chips—this is the stuff of celebration.

There are two approaches to celebrating. One is an escape from life. When loneliness becomes too painful to bear, when the wounds of life are fresh and deep, when love is a distant and hollow memory, people like to retreat into happy oblivion. They blot out life in its rawness and become fuzzy-headed with whatever drug takes their fancy. They throw themselves into loveless meetings of bodies, hoping that a tide of pleasure may fill the echoing caverns within. The barb of this type of partying is the morning after. You wake with a hairy tongue, aware that you have spent a little more of your dwindling self-esteem, and still having to face the pain you began with.

The mount of celebration in Godzone is quite the opposite. It is the intensifying of life—the celebration of life itself. It grows from a recognition of God present in every nook of experience. Birth, death, friendship, failure, ripening, love, redundancy, and arrival all become fuel to brighten the fire of celebration. If there be pain and loss, it is looked in the face and wailed into the night. When there is joy, it is woven into song and laughter and dancing that fills the halls of friendship.

Always there is food and drink. It may only be a packet of instant noodles washed down with coffee substitute, but it is shared. The sharing is the secret. Jesus had been talking to a huge crowd up in the hills. He figured they were getting hungry, so he called the disciples together and said, "Feed them." The disciples freaked. They explained as to a slow child that they only had a few fish and some stale bread, and they were feeling a little peckish themselves. Jesus taught them how to celebrate. He took what they had to offer, thanked God for it, and shared it. The rest is history.

To celebrate is to transform; it is to make the ordinary special—or perhaps it is to recognize the specialness of the ordinary. Sometimes a shaft of sunlight picks out an apple on a fruit bowl, and that apple becomes a gateway to the mystery of the universe. God is in every place and moment. Celebration opens our eyes so that we begin to see. As you sit around the table, suddenly there is another guest, another voice, another presence. Everything becomes crystal clear. At certain moments the walls fade and you are surrounded by a sea of faces, all lending their voices to the song. At those times you have climbed so high as to see clear beyond the horizon.

Valleys

It was a time like that when Jesus took a few of the disciples up to the heights of Godzone. In the midst of their talking, they became aware of Jesus glowing like a reactor. And then there were a few extra guests around the table, including Moses and Elijah, who had been certified dead some centuries before. The disciples began to wonder what was in the soup. Peter was so excited that he wanted to stay there forever. Running off at the mouth as usual, he suggested they build a few houses at the top of the mountain. It was so good he didn't ever want to come down again.

But mountaintops are not for living on. Once you've seen the lie of the land, you have to move on—and that means coming down. The journey takes place on the ground, where the road is. There is a certain wistfulness in leaving behind the peaks, but experienced trailblazers of Godzone have learned to hold in their heart what they learned on the heights, and to feed on it for many miles. There will be more mountains, but meantime the road leads on.

Often the way out of the mountains leads through valleys. In a valley the hills rise steeply on either side of the road, cutting out the sun and making it dark and cold. Free spirits who long for the open spaces can feel trapped in a valley. It's possible to become depressed, to lose faith that the road will ever lead out onto the plains again. The dankness seeps into the soul. It seems that one always travels through valleys alone, even if there are other people with you. Valleys are a part of the journey and have their own stark beauty.

Loss

How loss affects you depends on your relation to that which is lost. Few people mourn the loss of weight, but they may miss the hair that clogs the drain. When you have loved what you lose, a part of you goes with it. It may be your friend, your job, your dream, your cat, your lover. To be human is to experience loss, but that doesn't help you bear it. If a limb is torn from your body, you are as likely to die from shock as from loss of blood. It was there; now it is gone. The suddenness and finality of loss is the first black shadow as the sun disappears behind the ridge.

But the dark days are just beginning. Before you emerge into the light again you will be stripped to the core. You will rage and scream at God. You will retreat into a cocoon of sorrow and breathe in slow motion. The color will drain from the sky, the meaning from life. As a plow tears through hard earth, your heart will be broken up. You will make friends with pain, nursing it as the child of your grief. Utter emptiness fills the earth, and the valley appears to contain nothing but the echo of your own cry. Surely God has left you. The road that seemed to be heading somewhere has become a dead end. A mocking maze with no exit.

Then, one morning in the distant future, you wake and hear a bird singing. Nothing dramatic, but it is the first time for so long that you have actually heard. For a few moments, the tide of pain rolls back and you are aware of nothing but the song of the bird. It is the first ray of light to strike you as the foothills fall away at the mouth of the valley. Hardly daring to believe it, you are beginning to come out of the darkness. You walk out into the open a different person than the one who entered the valley. The shadow is now a part of you, a part of the journey, except that it is subsumed in life.

A woman was walking along the road, shoulder to shoulder with the Lord. They stopped beside an old gnarled tree and looked back. The woman could trace their footsteps in the dust from where they had come. Where the road entered the valley, one set of footprints abruptly stopped. The single trail continued until the mouth of the valley, where once again there were two sets side by side. She thought back to the pain of the valley. "Tell me, Lord," she said, "why did you leave me then when I needed you most?"

"Leave you?" he asked, bemused. "That's where I was carrying you."

Suffering

Happy-clappy Christians are free from misfortune. They are confident, successful, beautiful, and have fewer cavities. Lucky for them. Godzoners, on the other hand, endure the ravages of suffering. It sometimes seems that they get more than their fair dollop of it. Perhaps this is a part of sharing the life of God. The travelers of the Zone regularly get brain tumors, have miscarriages, run over the cat, and go to prison. Many have been tortured, persecuted, burned at the stake in the name of religion. To follow the road is not a bowl of roses, as Jesus demonstrated. It is to follow the road, even when it passes through the valley of the shadow of death.

Job (pronounced Jobe), being surprisingly both wealthy and good, was full of the joys of the Lord. In the space of twenty-four hours his life fell apart. The Sabeans rustled his cattle and killed the drovers. The Chaldeans took his camels and put their drivers to the sword. Lightning struck the barn during shearing time, and started a fire that wiped out his entire flock of sheep together with the shepherds. A tornado ripped through the house where all Job's sons and daughters were having a family reunion. The roof fell in and killed them all. Job, being a patient man, was inclined to think, "Tomorrow is the first day of the rest of my life," and leave it at that.

But then he got sick. His body erupted into painful boils, and he developed some form of leprosy. Job was beginning to feel that he had been given a raw deal. In a fit of self-pity, he beat what was left of his breast with what was left of his fists. He cursed the day of his birth and sent a few pertinent questions Godward. The only response was more suffering in the form of four friends who came to cheer him up and explain everything. Advice to the suffering is insufferable. When a person cries, "Why did this happen!" they do not want an answer. They want someone to hold them.

Job's friends regarded suffering as a form of punishment. In their collective wisdom, God blessed the good with wealth and punished the bad with suffering. It so happened that they were fairly well off themselves. Their logic was impeccable. God causes the wicked to suffer; Job is suffering; ergo: Job is wicked. They advised him to come clean and repent of his secret sins. It wasn't so much that Job recognized the fallacy of their major premise. He simply knew that far from being wicked, he had devoted his life to serving God. All he wanted was some reassurance that God was still around the place. In the end God put in a personal appearance, sent a few pertinent questions Jobward, and saw off the well-intentioned friends before anyone died of boredom.

A scholar who fancied himself a student of Zen noticed a man dozing by the riverbank. He crept up behind the man and gave him a solid whack across the back of the neck. The man woke angrily and rose to retaliate to this indignity.

"Hit me if you will," said the scholar, "But before you do, let me ask you a question. Was the sound of that smack the result of my hand that struck, or your neck that received the blow?"

The man replied, "Answer that yourself. My pain doesn't allow me to ask fancy questions. You can afford to do so only because you don't feel what I feel."

God does not cause suffering. God suffers suffering. Those who walk the road that leads to God participate in it as surely as a cheap hotel has bed bugs. To resist suffering is to cripple the spirit as well as the body. To roll with it does not lessen the pain, but makes of suffering a teacher, unwelcome yet formative. It is said of Jesus that, like us, he learned in the school of suffering. Those who have had their hearts gouged by suffering find that it provides a channel for a deep river to flow.

Though the sun does not shine in the valley, it is still there. Like a matron's view of her navel, it is simply hidden by the hills. If the valleys of Godzone be dark and frightening, they are as full of God as every other part of the road. Those traveling through them come out stronger and surer, more able to love without fear. They belong now to a fellowship of suffering, and will recognize others who have endured the valleys by something in their eyes. They will not say more than one or two words about it, but they will share a secret knowledge.

Lakes

The road gets tiring and dusty. We pilgrims love to be moving, but there are times on a hot afternoon when you stick to the plastic seat of a Plymouth and long for something cool and refreshing. To be dropped off beside a deep mountain lake; to rest your pack against a rock; to slowly remove your dust-white clothes; to step down to the shore and take a long cold drink; to dive into the still dark waters and shudder with shock; to feel the freshness washing over you and soothing out the weariness.

And then to climb out and lie on your back in the sun, letting your mind go blank, listening to the ever so gentle lapping of the water on the shore. You can feel the strength flooding back in, the hope and the purpose. A few hours later you're back on the side of the road again, sitting on your pack, as renewed as a forest by a rainfall. The water has cleansed, refreshed, restored you. It has not only washed the dust of the road off the outside, it has bathed the tired places on the inside.

You can get weary in Godzone too. When you do, you begin to look out for some place along the road to stop off and put yourself back together. Fortunately, the geography of Godzone is arranged in such a way that just when you need it, a deliciously inviting lake appears around the corner. The rest is there for the taking, and those who plan to keep moving onwards and upwards soon learn the importance of using it. A dip in the still waters clears your head and calms your heart, allows you to think again. It gets rid of the dirt of the world that has stuck to you in your travels.

The still water in Godzone is known as prayer. While the lakes of prayer are as varied as an alcoholic's excuses, all of them are places of refreshment. Prayer is the oasis on the road. It is the place of communion with God, where you open the intimate places of your heart and admit God. As you strip naked to swim in a lake, so you bare yourself in prayer. And as the cool water slakes, so prayer cleanses and recreates you.

The consumers of the world all want to know the how of prayer, and have created a market for how-to books. But do they really help? Does a sex manual with full color photos help two lovers tumbling through the rapids! With both prayer and sex, the depth of the experience depends not so much on technique as on love. Where the heart burns, it finds its own unique way to express its passion. God is not seeking a perfect performance, but a living relationship with you. Love will take you by the hand and lead you gently to the inner places.

In the Middle Ages there was a bishop in the Mediterranean who was responsible for a large territory. He heard one day of a very small community of Christians on a remote island, and determined to visit them to give them instruction.

He sailed to the barren outcrop of rock, and there discovered three fishermen who had come to faith through a shipwrecked traveler who had since died. They had no scriptures or liturgy. Their only prayer was this: "We are three; you are three. Have mercy on us." The bishop was pleased with their warmth and devotion, and began to give them some basic Christian teaching. In particular, he taught them how to pray the Lord's prayer. They had difficulty remembering it all, but finally the bishop was satisfied and took his leave.

As he was sailing back over the horizon, pleased with his day's work, the bishop noticed a tiny glowing light in the distance. He watched in astonishment as it grew closer and larger, and appeared to be heading directly toward his boat. He saw that it was a great ball of fire, and there in the center of the fire were the three fishermen, running across the top of the waves.

"Bishop," they called as they came alongside the boat, "Please forgive us. We have forgotten already how we are to pray."

"Go home," said the chastened bishop, "and return to the prayer that you know."

The lake of prayer is deeper than the fount of dreams. After paddling around on the surface for a while, most who have tasted begin to want more. They dive down into the water and discover that it is possible to breathe down there. The inner chambers are washed with light streaming from the depths. Far below the surface God waits, in a place where dreams are forged and the language is love. The movement of prayer is the slipping of a smooth pebble into the quiet waters.

For many of us the lake is polluted. Over a period of years we have thrown our rubbish into it, and now when we go looking for God it rises to meet us. Anger, fear, bitterness, grief—they have built up in the vaults and block our way to God. It is possible to ignore the junk that rises in prayer. But then, like a potholer in a volcano, you can go no deeper. To find the passion for which you hunger, the pool must be cleaned out, over and over again. It is worth the effort.

Prayer is a waste of time. A glorious waste of time! Time bathed in, time squelched through the fingers, time burrowed and frolicked in. Drifters are used to the jibe that they are wasting their lives, so one more example of their decadence brings no shame. In prayer it is possible to find the still center again, and out of the silence there comes the gentling voice of God. When you return to break the waters on the surface, you do it renewed. In the afterglow of love you saunter back to the road with a Mona Lisa smile, ready for the next adventure.

Rivers

Rivers sluice their way through Godzone, bearing life. Rivers, of course, are notoriously unpredictable. They will tickle your feet one day, and wash away the bridges the next. They change their course more times than the Chinese change their history. Rivers should no more be taken for granted than the orthodoxy of familiar slogans. Nevertheless, the dangerous vitality of rivers makes them exciting.

In Godzone the rivers are all streams of the flowing Spirit. They tumble through the dry places, bringing life and greenness in their wake. The Spirit is the harborer and nurturer of life. When the waters of the Spirit pass by, everything changes. You may have been sitting at the gate of a farm since six o'clock A.M. with only two cars gone past and no ride. The farmer trundles out to the gate on his tractor and says hello. He hands you a paper bag, saying, "We saw you sitting out here by the road and thought you might be hungry." Inside you find thick sandwiches, some boiled eggs, and an apple. The Spirit just flowed through.

For the most part, pilgrims of the Zone don't follow the rivers; they simply meet them where they cross the road. You can pass over bridges and hardly notice them, or you can stop and get your feet wet. Each river has something to teach, a gift to give. In order to learn and receive, you have to wade in and be prepared to be tossed around a little. Maybe you will be swept downstream. Perhaps you will come out at a different point than you went in. You can no more control a river than hurry a bureaucrat.

The currents of the Spirit are transforming the land. They wear away the resistance of rock, carving out gorges and canyons. They seduce and they storm, moody as a cat with PMS. One very deep stream of the Spirit is called justice. It is a mighty river, which flows out of the heart of Godzone. Some think they can dam it. But whether in South Africa or Chile, it will not be blocked. The more it is held back, the greater the pressure that builds up. Those who oppose it are swept away like feathers in a flood.

You can fill your water bottle from the river. The water you draw from it will keep you going for a while. Every time you take a swig of the pure sweetness of it, something of the river enters you. But you can't carry enough to last for always. You need to come back to the river time and time again. Each time it will be a different stream, but the same Spirit that flows through all of them. Zone travelers come to love the rivers, because they know the spring from which they bubble is the very heart of God.

The Ocean

The sea has a magnetic pull that affects more than tides. Who can forget the first sight of it after a long journey through the interior? Like an old friend, it is often left behind but never forgotten. The sea holds more memories than an old woman's jewelry box. Long walks along the beach to help you think. Watching the waves pound in on a gray and stormy day. Becoming a child again as you explore the rock pools for signs of life. Strange yearnings and dreamings as the moon hauls itself over the horizon.

The ocean is vast and heaving. Most of us only know its edges. We paddle in the shallow waters, or throw sticks for dogs into the waves. Even if we venture in to swim, we don't go out too far. There comes a point beyond the breakers where the sheer hugeness of the sea becomes overwhelming. The thought of how much water is beneath you can flood the imagination and make you scared. Even the massive waves worshipped by surfies are only ripples on the surface.

The sea that laps the coast of Godzone is the love of God. When it comes to bathing on these beaches, most of us have never had our feet off the bottom. Perhaps it is just as well. In a love as vast as this, we could drown as easily as a flea in a hot tub. There is a time for that, but not while we still have so far to travel. There is no harm in taking a few hours to sit on the shore and meditate on the meaning of marshmallow, sometimes perhaps to lie down at the water's edge and allow the sea to wash over you, to tug at you as it sucks back into the depths. One woman who did this wrote later, "You would know our Lord's meaning in this thing? Know it well. Love was the meaning. Who showed it you? Love. What did God show you? Love. Why were you shown it? For love. Hold on to this and you will know and understand love more and more. But you will not know or learn anything else—ever. So it was that I learned that love was God's meaning. And I saw for certain, both here and elsewhere, that before ever we were made, God loved us; and that this love has never slackened, nor ever shall. In this love all works have been done, and in this love God has made everything serve us; and in this love our life is everlasting. Our beginning was when we were made, but the love in which we were made never had beginning. In it we have our beginning."

Two travelers were walking by the edge of the sea. The younger one was tired and thirsty. He said to his old master, "I am thirsty."

The old man prayed, and then said, "Go ahead, drink from the sea."

The water turned out to be sweet and pure. The young man enjoyed it so much that he filled a flask from the ocean.

"What are you doing that for?" asked the old man, puzzled.

"It's so that I won't be thirsty later on," replied the novice.

The old man laughed. "God is here," he said, "and God is everywhere."

The Desert

The desert is a barren waste. It is long and flat and empty and bare. Hitchhikers generally avoid deserts because they are not healthy places to be stuck without a ride. But in Godzone the road passes sooner or later through the desert. Here there is a spiritual emptiness. Hope turns to sand in the mouth. You lose the sense of where it was you were heading to. Your cry for God comes echoing back to you on the wind, mocking.

And then as the darkness enters your heart like a chill blade, the beasts come out—monsters bent on tearing you apart. The desert is the place of temptation, and as in backstreet Cairo, you have to keep your wits about you to survive. The ghouls come to terrify or seduce. There is nothing more to draw on in defense than what you have brought with you. It is a struggle in which you face the truth of yourself, like a look in the mirror on the morning after. Only late in the piece do you become aware that the monsters you are battling all have your face. They are the shadow side of you, safely contained on the highways, but exposed and dangerous in the desert wastes.

Immediately after his baptism, Jesus was led out into the desert, where he fasted for forty days and forty nights. The devil came to him in his hunger and weakness, whispering sweet temptations in his ear.

"If only, if only," simpered Satan.

Jesus' hunger made him vulnerable, open to a different voice. Nevertheless, he resisted and overcame the devil. Shortly afterward Jesus came out of the desert knowing his mission, and with the Sermon on the Mount on his lips. The temptation had stripped him bare, and all that was left was bedrock.

The desert is not only a wilderness but a place of beauty. Out of it spring exotic flowers of creativity, poetry that hooks the gut, dreams that change the shape of the world. The total emptiness of the desert hammers out new characters on its barren anvil. Travelers come out of it with purpose in their hearts and thunder in their voices. The inner monsters are tamed and impotent, because they have been faced down. The dreaded wastes have become fertile, and are forever more remembered by the nomad as a space haunted with loveliness.

The road leads on and out, further in and further up. You can learn the lie of the land, but never finish exploring the realm of Godzone. True to the drifter's itch, there is always one more place along the way to discover. The road that leads into town has a matching road that leads out, and comfortable as you might become, you can never quite settle while the journey remains unfinished. You may reach the edge, but not the end of the Zone. It is still being created; God can't quite settle either.

No one can give you a detailed map for your travels; all they can do is to tell their own tales of the road. Even the valleys and deserts and peaks will only become known as you experience them for yourself. The key to finding your way is to trust the road. Don't leave it when it goes through hard places. Return to it when the wonders of some sight have drawn you aside. When it winds back on itself, there is a reason. There are no shortcuts to be taken, no helicopter rides to lift you out of trouble. The road has its own wisdom, and the followers of it arrive eventually at their next destination, with many new stories to share.

4

CUSTOMS

In a new land you get street-smart or you get ripped off. There are always twenty small boys tugging at your sleeves, offering to sell "zero-zero" hashish, their sister, or a splinter of the one true cross. They have naive travelers for breakfast. Old hands pick up survival techniques, like dividing the asking price by ten to begin haggling. Or learning enough local language to say, "I have lice," and, "Where is the toilet?" You slowly appreciate the finer points of particular cultures and refrain from asking for a ham sandwich in Jerusalem or a rubber in America.

Language and culture unlock the mysteries of strange and wonderful countries. Those who don't attempt to learn them might as well have stayed home and watched a travelogue on television. Without a working knowledge of local customs, the explorer is as welcome as an auditor to a tainted televangelist.

True travelers come to learn, unlike colonists, who come to conquer. To understand, there is no substitute for time with the people. However, you may pick up a few basic tips in advance to save from making a bigger fool of yourself than necessary. Because Godzone has no boundaries, the travelers of the Zone are recognized in the main by their customs. Before Christianity got sponsored and turned into a religion, it used to be called "the Way." The friends of Jesus, those who saw God through him, were known as the followers of the Way. They were people who not only fronted the road, but who sought to live according to the ways of the Zone. They looked to Jesus as a pioneer, an ambassador from the heartland who could teach the language and lifestyle that would equip them in their journey to the center.

In determining whether someone is a pilgrim of the Zone, what they do is always more important than what they say. Words are produced at minimal cost. Actions are personally expensive. Two kids watching television were asked to lend a hand with the dishes. One said, "Sure thing. I'll be right there. Dishes are no trouble to me; I even enjoy doing them. No sweat." But the program got interesting so he never quite got to the sink. The other, a teenage daughter, said, "Push off! I'm watching my favorite show." But at the first commercial break, she got up and did them all. Question: which one did what was asked? Some people sell package tours to Godzone who have never left their armchair in suburbia. Others who claim they don't know where they are going are experienced sojourners hiking the roads of Godzone without being aware of it. One of the first rules of survival in the Zone is to take nothing at face value. The culture turns conventional ways of thinking upside down and inside out. But the things people do will tell you a lot about what is in their hearts. Committed Godzoners are easily recognized once you know what you're looking for.

Currency

American dollars proclaim to all the world, "In God We Trust." They are then used to pay for nuclear weapons that destroy people and the world itself. This is what is sometimes called blasphemy. Pilgrims of Godzone use any old currency, whether it carries a picture of Quaddafi or Mickey Mouse. The difference is they really trust in God. They know that funny-colored pieces of paper can't buy anything that really matters. But like everything else, money can be used for good or bad. People in the Zone carry purses and wallets, but they hold them loosely. The real currency they keep in their hearts, where it is easily got at and also protected from inflation.

Money is only a tool. You can use it to help you and others along the road, or it can use you and keep you so busy you never travel anywhere. Money makes a good servant but a poor lover.

A capitalist was horrified to find a fisherman lying beside his boat, smoking a pipe.

"Why aren't you out fishing?" he asked.

"Because I have caught enough fish for the day."

"Why don't you catch some more?" the capitalist persisted.

"What would I do with it?" asked the fisherman.

"Earn more money. Then you could have a motor fixed to your boat and go into deeper waters and catch more fish. That would bring you money to buy nylon nets, so more fish, more money. Soon you would have enough to buy two boats . . . even a fleet of boats. Then you could be rich like me.

"What would I do then?" asked the fisherman.

"Then you could really enjoy life," the capitalist replied.

"What do you think I am doing now?" responded the fisherman, refilling his pipe.

In the world at large, the smart thing to do with money is to hoard it in dark places, in the hope that it will breed. It does; it breeds greed. In Godzone the economy works in reverse. People who are on the move can't hoard anything. The trick is to give as much of your money away as possible. All that you give from love goes into Godbank. When you end up a long way down the road with barely enough to pay for the lettuce leaf of a hamburger, it comes back to you. You don't have to worry about deposit slips or interest rates or credit facilities. If you live by giving, you receive when you need it.

When parents put their kids through school, they want them to concentrate on study rather than how the bills will be paid. God wants us to pay attention to the road and its lessons, rather than incidentals like food and clothing. Look at the sparrows, said Jesus. They don't clock in each morning. They don't pay superannuation. They haven't even got a social welfare system. But they always have enough to eat. And see the flowers. They don't go to designer boutiques or visit Paris fashion shows. Yet the beauty and color of them would have made Princess Di green with envy. And you travelers of the Zone are every bit as valued as the birds and flowers.

But you can't operate both systems at once. You either trust God to look after you or you trust in yourself. It's no use expecting Godbank to come to the rescue when you have a little nest-egg term deposit at First National Bank of Security. You have to let go of the trapeze before you find out whether the safety net works.

Giving is a way of letting go. It is also a sign of trust in God. Like any lover, God likes to be trusted. It gives God the fun of thinking up interesting ways of providing what you need. Most times it involves fellow pilgrims, and so teaches us we are related to each other.

A man walking through the forest saw a fox that had lost its legs and wondered how it lived. Then he saw a tiger come with game in its mouth. The tiger had his fill and left the rest for the fox. The next day too God sent the tiger to feed the fox. The man began to wonder at God's greatness and thought, "I too shall lie in a corner trusting the Lord to give me all I need." He did this for a month, and was almost at death's door when he heard a voice that said, "Oh, you who are on the path of error, open your eyes to the Truth! Imitate the tiger, not the fox."

Giving keeps you in harmony with God, and so brings joy. The air you breathe comes free, water falls from the sky, beauty is not user-pays. Life itself is a gift, one to be valued and nurtured. Those who tune their lives to that of the Giver learn to keep their palms open. That way they can both give and receive. People who clench their fists to keep what they have are unable to take anything that is offered. And tragically, they often crush the life from what they grip so tightly.

There are those who try to turn a profit from Godzone. These entrepreneurial evangelists hear the story of God's generosity and determine to become wealthy through manipulating it. You will meet them on the road, selling their get-rich systems while quoting Bible verses. They were enough to get Jesus really hacked off when he booted them out of the Temple. God provides for needs, not materialist fantasies. The riches of Godzone are such that you cannot lose them by giving them away: peace, freedom, contentment, love, acceptance.

Sharing is a way of life in the Zone. There is a healthy recognition that nothing can be "Owned." There was once an American tourist who went to visit the Spanish author of many profound books. He was astonished to discover that the great writer's home was a simple shack filled with books. The only furniture was a table and a chair.

"Where is your furniture?" asked the tourist.

"Where is yours?" countered the author.

"Mine? But I'm only passing through. I'm a visitor here."

"So am I," said the writer.

Language

Words are a way of bringing out what is on the inside of a person. There are hundreds of languages and millions of words, but a limited number of things to be carried by them. Though it is true that Arabic offers a great variety of ways in which to curse your enemy, the feeling expressed is common to all peoples. Godzonese is not a language of the lips, but a language of the heart. It can be spoken in Italian or Samoan, and heard by the deaf. Once you have learned its basics, it will serve you wherever the road may lead.

It is about speaking the truth in love. Speaking the truth is hard enough. We play word games to disguise our true feelings.

"That's a lovely jacket; it's so simple." (I'm jealous that you can afford to buy new clothes.)

"Thank you. I picked it up in Singapore." (I'm a jet-setting beautiful person, na-na-na.)

"I've heard they have such cheap clothes there." (Take that, you stuck-up troll.)

"I never bother about the price of things, do you?" (I'm rich enough not to care, while you can't afford a trip to the toilet.)

"Oh no, dear, only the quality." (Which is why I wouldn't be seen dead in that hideous jacket.)

Lying is so common we call it politeness. It pollutes the stream of conversation. Often it's hard to tell what is true from what is false. We begin to believe our own lies. When somebody speaks the plain truth it stands out like a hitchhiker at a charity ball. The truth is painful to speak and brings conflict in a world that lives by deception. Jesus was crucified for his troubles. Nobody wants their precious illusions torn, their nakedness exposed. It is easier to continue pretending and execute those who won't play.

To speak the truth in love is even more difficult. To stab with a knife is easy; to cut with a scalpel in order to heal requires skill and restraint. Truth may be spoken without love, just as love may be built without truth. The language of Godzone brings them together in such a way as to create life and hope and freedom for those who hear. It is a language free from flattery, gossip, innuendo, and bitter criticism. It is scented with the breath of God, and able to change reality.

When water is muddied, it becomes clear again by allowing it to stand still. The language of Godzone arises from silence and stillness. Noise clouds it, chattering stirs the pool to opacity. As with any language, Godzonese is first learned by listening. In the deep spaces between the notes, the voice of God comes. It is heard with the heart, not the ears. One word is enough to water arid wastes, to heal bruised flesh, to rekindle smoldering ashes. It can transform whoever receives it.

The language of Godzone springs from such transformed hearts. It is never to be spoken to another until it has been addressed to oneself. Jesus pointed out our tendency to put our friends through the sifter looking for mouse dirt, when our own feet are deep in elephant crap. What is on the inside of us comes out in the way we speak, whether we like it or not. We speak either the language of deceit and hatred or that of truth and love. The one cripples and destroys; the other redeems and creates.

Words are like arrows; once they have been sent on their way they can no more be recalled than a rabbit can be celibate. Vindictive words pierce and wound, and apology will not remove the scars they cause. Many children are fatally wounded by their parents. Words such as "stupid" or "ugly" take root in the heart and grow quietly until they have choked the life out of any healthy plants that may have existed. By the same token, words like "beautiful" or "precious" make the heart's soil rich and fertile, capable of producing much fruit. As a river can be traced by the green slash hemming its path, so those fluent in the language of Godzone leave love in their wake.

Lifestyle

People in warm sunny places laugh a lot, are expansive, and don't worry too much about time. Those in colder climates are more cautious, analytical, and industrious. Which is to say that everyone is affected by their environment. Travelers of the Zone, of course, are on the move, and so not deeply shaped by weather. But they do reflect their habitat in the way they live. They breathe the air of Godzone, and so their lives waft its fragrance through the world. They come in all shapes and sizes and colors, but like intruders at a nudist colony, there are certain distinctive things that mark them out from the crowd. Lifestyle is the passport of a true citizen of Godzone. Many claim to be residents because of birth or belief but contradict this by living according to a different code.

There is no dual citizenship in the Zone. You opt in or out, and your decision is displayed for all to see in how you shape your life. Apple trees do not produce onions, and thistle bushes do not bear figs. At least they didn't before the days of genetic engineering. In the same way, the truth of a person is revealed in what their life produces, not in the label on the packet.

Simplicity

Godzoners live simple lives, lives uncluttered with knick-knacks or philosophies. As a rule, they do not collect, hoard, consume, or preserve. Their needs are few and simple, their words honest and considered, their friendship genuine and warm. Through a trail of imaginative failures they have learned to love people and use things, rather than loving things and using people. They do not require large amounts of food to be satisfied, money to be content, or praise to be secure. All of life is an adventure playground to them, and they have kept their childlike sense of awe in an age of lost innocence.

The pilgrims of the Zone have cleared the house of their spirit so that it is barer than a nun's hope chest. That way they can make room for God and for others. They live lives of welcome and hospitality, where there is always room at the table for one more. The loaf of bread will not be diminished by being shared; the jug of wine will easily warm another's belly. The few valuables of people exploring Godzone are stories, jokes, and songs, and these are free to any who will hear them.

Jesus is to many of these raconteurs both teacher and friend. They take seriously his advice to give up their wealth, to have purses that don't wear out, to give to those who ask, to speak plainly and truly, to trust God rather than worry, not to retaliate against violence, to cleanse the inside before the outside. If he had only mouthed off, they would be suspicious of him. But he lived the life, and through it shone a simplicity and singlemindedness as compelling as a garbage bag to a hungry dog.

Because they are not distracted by the cacophony of demands that fills the earth, the explorers of the Zone develop the ability to focus. In the hype and hysteria of modern life, they clear a channel through the verbal diarrhea. Godzoners are not fooled by Politicospeak or swayed by the Mindbenders. The river of their lives is not decanted into a hundred shallow streams, but flows deep and slow, the unrelenting surge belied by a calm surface.

It is a simplicity not of thickness but of breadth; not of ignorance but of goodness. None of them would claim that for themselves. But years of following the road, of listening intently, of emptying themselves of all but love, has meant that something of God shines from their lives. They have a presence about them that makes you want to confide all your secrets and doubts. With disarming warmth, they put you at ease. If you are close to the Zone yourself, you will be drawn to them as a mosquito to warm flesh. To those, however, who are still running from God, these nomads with the distinctive reek of the beyond will be more alarming than a Reagan comeback.

Gratitude

Sometimes gratitude can be fawning. We have all met people who exude grease like they were planning to swim the Atlantic. If Godzoners are grateful, it is not that they curry favor or say thank you all the time. It is more like a profound thankfulness in the way they live, the way they laugh, the way they share. Because they know the Giver, they recognize the giftedness of all that comes, both good and bad. All of life is an opportunity for enjoyment or learning, and they are determined to catch what's drifting past like shooters bagging clay-pigeons.

Their lifestyle demonstrates it. They are forever finding an excuse to celebrate—making of half a chance a party, drawing out the specialness of a person, hearing the lyrics of a new song in a poignant phrase. It is a spontaneous combustion of the heart, a recognition of the all-pervading presence of God, which cannot be contained. When Jesus rode into Jerusalem, the rabble whooped it up so much that the preservers of propriety wanted them to shut up. "If they were to keep quiet," said Jesus, "the stones themselves would let rip."

He was right. There is a deep hum of thanksgiving throbbing in the universe. When Godzoners give voice to their gratitude, they are picking up the tune. Their cracked crooning may not win any talent quests, but it blends perfectly in the greater rhapsody. All that has life and knows God joins in. This fugue of thanksgiving, when it is wrung from a life, transforms the world. It brings God out of the wings and onto center stage.

A humble peasant took a trip to a strange land. He took an ass, a rooster, a few books of poetry, and a lamp. Since he was so poor he was refused hospitality in the village inns and forced to sleep in the woods. He lit his lamp to read before going to sleep. But a fierce wind came up, knocking over the lamp and breaking it. So he decided to turn in, saying, "Thanks be to God who does all things well." During the night some wild animals came along and drove away the rooster, and thieves stole the ass. The man woke up, saw the loss, but still proclaimed easily, "Thanks be to God who does all things well."

He then went back to the village where he was refused lodging only to learn that enemy soldiers had invaded it during the night and killed all the inhabitants. He also learned that these same enemy soldiers had traveled through the same part of the woods where he lay asleep. Had his lamp not blown out he would have been seen. Had not the rooster been chased it would have crowed, giving him away. Had not the ass been stolen it would have brayed. So once more he said, "Thanks be to God who does all things well!"

Acceptance

Those who have discovered for themselves the way in which God loves them, find accepting others as natural as nightfall. God has overlooked so much in their lives that the least they can do is return the favor. Such refugees from condemnation are not inquisitors or referees. They take people as they come, looking for the truth, the spark of God within every person. Faults and failings are ignored as distortions, the rough surface of an uncut diamond. Zone-dwellers tend to attract people who are the outcasts of society; Jesus was known as the friend of bludgers, deadbeats, crooks, and no-hopers.

He was always prepared to bend the rules where people were concerned. This was unpopular with the Divine Law Enforcement Agency, who operate the moralistic strings that keep the puppets dancing. Here is a fable at their expense.

God walked into heaven and discovered that everyone was there. This didn't seem fair, as some of them had done terrible things in life. So everyone was summoned before God, where an angel read the ten commandments. When the first commandment was read, God said, "Everyone who has broken this commandment will have to leave." The same happened with each of the other commandments. By the time the angel had finished reading the seventh, there was hardly anyone left. God looked up and saw a small group of grim self-righteous ascetics looking very smug. For a few minutes God considered the prospect of eternity with them, and then shouted out, "All right everyone, come back!" The religious group were furious, saying "We have wasted our lives."

Acceptance grows from the deliberate short-sightedness of love. It recognizes that one word of encouragement to a fragile person is worth more than a thousand lectures on their faults. Acceptance provides the air that makes it possible for a strangled life to breathe and grow again.

"I was a neurotic for years. Anxious, depressed, selfish. And everyone kept telling me to change. I resented them, and agreed with them, and wanted to change, but simply couldn't, no matter how I tried. What hurt the most was that, like the others, my closest friend kept urging me to change. So I felt powerless and trapped. One day she said to me,

"Don't change. I love you as you are." These words were music to my ears: "Don't change. Don't change. Don't change . . . I love you as you are." I relaxed. I came alive. And suddenly, I changed!"

The profound gratitude of Godzoners is closely linked to their heart-felt acceptance. They have been forgiven so much that they hardly even see the failings of others. Like beggars at a banquet, the only thing that would make them happier is to have their mates tuck in alongside them.

Serving

Most people who want to get ahead do it through ambition, greasing, backstabbing, and crawling. Their sense of importance is bolstered by the number of subordinates they can boss around.

When two followers of Jesus began to argue about who was the most important, he explained to them how the system works in Godzone. "Whoever wants to be chief-wallah in the Zone," he said, "must become the slave of all." In case they hadn't quite got the message, he later took a bowl of water and a towel and washed their smelly feet. That made it easier for them to remember.

The pilgrims of the Way spend their lives learning how to be good servants. With dignity and a sense of understanding, they perform such grandiose tasks as cleaning toilets and pulling nose hairs. They do it not grudgingly but in joy, knowing that the one they truly serve is God. Even so, it is hardly surprising that Godzone holds little appeal for the rich and famous. They have so much to lose. They may get their hands dirty. People who are empty, on the other hand, find in serving a channel for their love. It is their means of feeling their way into the life of God.

Freddie the cockroach didn't accept that this was his station in life. So one day when his guardian angel appeared, he didn't take long to decide what wish to have.

"Make me into a human," he said, "so I can have more power." With Spielberg side-effects, he became human and was the office boy in a big publishing firm.

He soon got sick of making cups of tea and sharpening pencils. He called back the angel, and demanded to become much more important. Instantly Freddie was the office manager, with a staff working for him. But he couldn't stop thinking that he was only on the third floor of the building, and there were seven more floors above him.

Summoning the angel once again, he asked this time to become the most important person in the firm. Straight away he was seated behind a huge desk in the executive office of Managing Director. This suited Freddie well, and he reveled in the authority and decision-making power he wielded. But looking out the window at the changing weather, he realized that he was still not top of the heap. There was One more above him. The angel was by now somewhat reluctant to answer Freddie's insistent call and assured him this would be the last wish.

"Make me into God," said Freddie. When he opened his eyes, he was a cockroach again.

Hope

Death comes early to those who slam the door of the future and resign themselves to living comfortably in the cell of their own making. Drifters find it hard to understand the surrender of suburbanites to mediocrity. Surely they still have roads untraveled, dreams as yet not pursued. Hope is the tug of the unknown, the lure to move out of the familiar present, the snatch of music that creates a hunger to hear more. It permeates the lives of Godzoners like the aroma of warm bread, making of them pilgrims and dreamers to eternity.

The idea of fate is bad karma. Those who subscribe to it become passive and powerless. Their blood coagulates in their veins; their bones become stiff and brittle. Life requires risk; it requires adventure, experiment, possibility. In short, life requires hope. It is hope that fuels the engine of creativity. It transforms the closed circle of conformity into an open spiral of potential.

It is not an empty escapist hope; it is not a "pie in the sky when you die" hope that retreats from reality. It is a hope full of substance. It works with the raw material of the here and now, but is not content to let it be. There is always the vision of what yet might be. Such hope is infectious. "I have a dream," says Martin Luther King, and suddenly we can all see that dream with him. Hope is the barb on the hook of God, and it holds us fast while we are yanked into the Zone.

Pioneers of the heartland live in such a way as to create hope for all those they meet. With the rainbow flash in their lives, they remind the inmates of Graytown that there is color in the universe. People whose senses have grown dull find the nagging ache of buried dreams soon returns when they sit at table with such pilgrims. For at least that time the fog lifts and the mountains beckon. They find themselves now able to believe what had earlier seemed cruel and taunting. Some will shake themselves out of it and return next morning to the safety of normality. But others will notice that the door they had always thought locked now stands ajar and walk through it, never to return.

Purpose

The fond illusion of bureaucrats and boffins is that travelers are wasting their lives. They imagine that because we keep on moving, we are drifting without aim. Little do they know that every journey has a destination, and that our movement is because we can't let go of the voyage of discovery we have begun. This compulsion is every bit as strong in the Zone. All who follow the road are as filled with purpose as a Mormon on a mission. They know that should they pitch camp in some layby and give up the pilgrimage, that particular path that was theirs to follow will remain untraveled.

In every score written by Mozart, each note is significant. You can't leave any note out because it doesn't fit on the page. Editing destroys the flow and mood; the whole work will shudder like a malarial speed freak. God has composed a piece that uses the entire human race. Its fullness and majesty needs all to become what they are, to sound true and clear and at the right pitch. No one can take the part of another, or improve the music by shifting their key.

The journey of Godzoners is driven by longing. Like pubescent Picassos, they hunger to express that which is within them. They scan the subtitles, search for signs, listen between the notes in order to know more clearly their purpose. They don't see the whole picture at the beginning of the adventure. But they frequently consult the compass to find out which direction to head in next. Once they have learned the next destination on the road, they head for it like accountants seeking a balance. Not until they have reached it do they start to consider the road beyond. Sometimes they hear whispers of their final destination but keep such insights quietly to themselves.

Jesus knew at an early stage that there was a cross waiting for him in Jerusalem. His friends warned him off cocking a snook at the establishment, but he knew he was heading the way God had called him to go. It didn't distract him from giving himself fully to the wastrels and vagabonds along the way. But there was fire in his bones and a hammer in his heart, and he set his face toward Jerusalem. Those who were game enough he called to follow, not to take his place but to keep him company.

The travelers of Godzone follow still. They have given up any trivial pursuits for the one aim of walking and working with God. The purpose of God consumes them, becomes their food and drink. They can't settle in any town along the way, because the time for resting has not come. The future calls, rampant and invasive. Nomads of the spirit succumb, and like a snail track on concrete, the path they wend through life glistens and shines behind them.

Justice

In order to love kids equally, you have to treat them differently. This, as the masseuse said to her client, is because they come in all types. God is fairer than a Quaker quartermaster, but as long as there is injustice in the world, some will get more attention than others. God has a special bias to the little people, the ones who get habitually done over. The poor, the disabled, the unloved, and the unlovely all find favor with God. In the Who's Who of the Zone, the order is topsy-turvy. The small and weak and vulnerable are the most highly regarded. The clever and powerful and beautiful can look out for themselves.

Travelers in the heartland, being in tune with the heart of God, understand this instinctively. They are friends of the poor, mostly themselves having become poor for the sake of God. But they are also campaigners for justice. They can't sit on their hands and watch while the weak are exploited, the different excluded, the powerless enslaved. When the mills of oppression begin to grind the poor, there you will find one or two of them, standing with the victims, crying out in the name of God against such abuse. Many of them are chewed up in the process, but this does not daunt them. Having given all to God, they have nothing left to lose.

Like earwigs, the merchants of injustice like to work in darkness. Godzoners will not let them. They overturn stones and go into the dark places, bringing a light that exposes the truth for all to see. The parasites scuttle away, finding a new crevice in which to spin their misery. But the sky is lightening as the dawn of Godzone creeps closer, and soon there will be no more hiding places left. Vermin beware!

Mercy

Let the final word be mercy. It needs no explanation.

5

DANGERS

The worst effects of danger are on those who least expect it. A wayfarer who tucks into a bowl of Mexican chili thinking that it's mince without the toast is in for a big shock. Innocents abroad either don't stay innocent for long, or don't stay abroad for long. Road-wise travelers are wily. They develop deep-set eyes with which to suss out dicey situations. While fun-loving and gregarious, they retain a quiet working suspicion geared toward survival. It gets them out of trouble.

That is not to say our lives are trouble-free. We explorers of life have tuned the radar of caution through manifold scrapes and hassles. We have had our packs stolen, out trust betrayed, our naiveté exposed. This is the baptism of the road, which sorts out the travelers from the tourists. Those who survive gain an inoculation of danger—a dose small enough not to kill, but strong enough to promote a lifelong resistance. Among nomads there are only the two types—the quick and the dead.

Godzone is full of danger. The unwary become unwell. "Be innocent as doves," Jesus advised, "and crafty as serpents." The deeper you penetrate into the heartland of the Zone, the greater and more subtle the dangers become. Road casualties abound. If you choose to follow the Way, there are certain events you can prepare yourself for that will help you to survive. Fellow travelers will assist you wherever they can, but there are always times when you are alone and vulnerable. A little preparation can save much discomfort and anxiety.

Evil

Evil is real. At times it holocausts to the surface, and then dives deep again. When people cannot see it, they laugh in its face. As ducklings are snaffled by eels, these laughing liberals are dragged under to be consumed. Science and sophistication provide no protection from the gnashing teeth of evil. They give it the camouflage to cruise without recognition. A duck that never puts its head below the water believes the world is calm and sunny. Those who say otherwise are scaremongers and spoilsports.

The great contribution of civilization is to create a facade to conceal the abattoirs of evil. But like jonquils in a john, it merely disguises that which it covers. A facelift may raise your bellybutton, but it does not delay death. And the ancient visage of evil is not made any safer by cosmetic improvements to its image. The less obvious that evil is, the more effective. These days it wears a suit and tie, sits in the boardroom, and has impeccable manners. Experienced travelers recognize it at once, simply by looking into the eyes.

Here is a letter from the wife of a doctor who was conducting experiments on the inmates of Dachau.

"Highly esteemed Reichsführer,

"You have given us great pleasure once again! So many good things! The children's evening porridge will be enriched now for quite a while. Heinrich Peter always fidgets with excitement when a parcel arrives. He guessed who had sent it and was of course given some chocolate immediately. Dear Reichsführer, I thank you from the bottom of my heart for the presents and the pleasure which you have given to us all. My husband is very fond of chocolate and took some with him to the concentration camp . . . At Easter he conducted the experiments, for which Dr. Romberg would have shown too much restraint and compassion, on his own."

Evil is more than simply the absence of good, just as darkness is more than simply the absence of light. Doing wrong things and even bad things takes no great effort, and we have all clocked up our share. But there comes a point when the bad deed is repeated without remorse, when the lie is retold until it is orthodoxy. It is then that a mysterious transition takes place, and wrong becomes evil, the lie takes life to itself. Evil is "live" spelled backwards, and it is the perversion of life. It exists only by sucking the marrow from its host body.

Evil has no life in itself; it is a parasite. It depends on finding a home in living beings. But once it has found a clawhold, it grows and spreads until it has consumed its unwitting carrier. In this way evil destroys itself, because it continually wipes out the basis of its existence. This does not stop it; evil is driven by appetite rather than intelligence. It attacks life as a fox attacks chickens, with a frenetic fury out of proportion to hunger. The unsuspecting are ripped apart before they have time to repeat the Rationalist's rosary.

The central target of evil is God. It thrives on perverting and corrupting every sign of God within the universe. The methodology is consistent. It takes what is good and twists until it becomes destructive. Love turns to lust, pleasure to perversion, passion to possession. The signs of its presence are envy, domination, hatred, addiction, deception, seduction, and fear. Creativity becomes technology, imagination becomes fantasizing, faith becomes religion. In this way evil seeks to remove the evidence of God from the world.

Evil stalks the paths of Godzone, like a pederast seeking to ravage all who pass by. Godzoners are welcome victims, because God's light shines in them. They attract the attention of the sinister forces as a hitchhiker does police cars. Evil has no real power over the sort of life they share, but tries desperately to keep this a secret. If through fear or distraction one of these sojourners can be delayed on the road, something has been achieved. Beginning travelers therefore need to learn the reality of evil, and the limits of its power.

A favorite ploy of evil is temptation. Unsummoned thoughts come hovering into consciousness. They tease and tantalize, whispering empty promises and plausible deceptions. They play on the weakness of the person they attack. The druggie contemplates a cleaner high, the lover a different partner, the dealer a shortcut to wealth. We cannot stop these thoughts flying across our heads, but, as a flat-nosed monk once said, we can certainly prevent them from building nests in our hair.

To relax concentration and allow the thought a crevice to sink into is to court disaster. It burrows deep into the psyche, looking for some warm and rotting compost to raise its maggot offspring in. The temptation grows stronger and more strident, leeching energy from healthy passions. Eventually, unable to be contained, it becomes a deed. The deed repeats itself and becomes a habit. The habit, fully blown, consumes the life.

The best way to defeat evil is to pursue good, or as those in the know prefer, to pursue God. There is a paradox in the existence of evil. Just as ignorance of its reality encourages its growth, so undue attention to it enlarges its sphere of activity. Evil is in essence a nothingness, a shadow created by the light. Wherever the presence of God is, the shadows of darkness dissolve. Travelers learn that by keeping their feet on the road and their minds on God, evil is repelled. To attack evil is to give it life, to walk towards it with trust and confidence is to overcome it.

Religion

A great explorer once returned to her people. They were eager to know all about her adventures, and in particular about the mighty Amazon, which she had traveled. But how could she speak of the feelings that had flooded her heart when she saw exotic flowers and heard the night sounds of the forests; when she sensed the danger of the wild beasts or paddled her canoe over treacherous rapids? She said to the people, "Go and find out for yourselves." To guide them she drew a map of the river.

They pounced upon the map. They framed it in their town hall. They made copies of it for themselves. They studied it night and day and became experts in interpreting the river. They knew its every turn and bend, they knew how broad it was, how deep, where the rapids and the waterfalls were. And yet not one of them ever left the village to see the river for themselves.

There are those who know Godzone and those who know about Godzone. Those who know about it know nothing. That does not stop them explaining it to all who will listen. They make faith into a structure called religion, and then climb inside to hide from God. It is a building without windows, tied together with laws and founded on pride. It contains priests and altars and sacred objects, but is careful to exclude God. The residents fashion a tame god in their own image, which can be more easily controlled than the Real One.

Such charlatans got right up Jesus' nose. "Don't do what they do," he warned, "for they preach but they don't deliver. They bind heavy burdens onto people's backs, but they themselves won't lift a finger to help. They do everything in public so that they will be seen, making long prayers and boring everyone silly. Hypocrites! They guard the gates of Godzone against pilgrims, neither going in themselves nor letting anyone else past. They are like up-market tombs with a brick and tile exterior, containing nothing but putrid corpses."

This fairly strong language was reserved for religious types who have long faces and who are so holy they fear mixing with mortals. Religion is a side track for those who like to pretend they are exploring the Zone while staying put. The problem is that it takes over the words and signposts of Godzone without their reality. Religious types and prissy puritans claim to represent God, effectively discouraging anyone other than wimps and undertakers from inquiring further. They represent more of a threat to the Zone than the most militant of atheists.

Religion is a danger to the greenhorns of Godzone. They may be misled by the words used and funneled off the road into the huge holding pens of the pious. They may mistake the words and rules for the reality. The halls of holiness are very comfortable, with their cushioned seating and shagpile carpet. Who would blame a weary traveler for preferring their comfort and security to the rigors of the road? Soothing sounds of piety and devotion can be seductive to one who began eager to follow and learn. But they do not satisfy.

A young boy went bike-riding out into the country. He did not pack any lunch, thinking to buy something along the way. He had cycled many miles and was suffering hunger pangs when he arrived in a small village. He spied outside a shop a sign that had a picture of a filled roll. It looked magnificent, with salami and cheese and tomato and pickles. His mouth already began to water as he stepped up to the counter.

"I'd like one of those rolls," he said to the shopkeeper. The man looked puzzled for a few seconds, and then laughed.

"This is not a food shop," he said. "We just paint signs."

Many hungry wayfarers have been turned away empty from the extravagant signs of religion. They promise much but deliver nothing. Hypocrisy is false advertising. It is better to say nothing than to mislead honest seekers. Genuine Godzoners need periodically to check themselves for the symptoms of hypocrisy. Whenever they become smug about their own progress, disapproving of others' morals, or just generally up themselves, preventative measures should be taken.

Fear

Fear can be quite sensible. It is appropriate to be afraid of putting your head out a train window, or your nose in a friend's quarrel. There is nothing wrong with being scared while climbing a rock face; it does wonders to assist concentration on the task at hand. But fear, like evil, often takes on a life of its own. Then it floods the mind and paralyzes the will, oblivious to any cause for its existence. Shadows become monsters, questions threats, silence terror. Fear forces people indoors, where they bolt and double-bolt the doors.

This sort of fear has an internal source. It is projected onto the world from the images in the heart. It populates Godzone with wild beasts and nameless horrors. Those who see them become stopped in their tracks and run frantically looking for shelter. It is no help to point out that these specters are not real. They are real to the person who sees them It is simply that the reality is embedded in the spirit rather than the environment.

Such fears are crippling. While they remain anonymous they loom large and all-powerful, towering tidal waves of terror. The only way past is to look them in the eye, to face them and learn their names. To take a step toward your fear is to find it diminish like a punctured ego. To walk right through it is to see it evaporate. For the person attempting this, it is akin to fronting up to a fast-moving twenty-ton truck. It can only be done out of a place of deep trust, and often with the help of a friend at each shoulder.

A demon decided to distract a man who was hurrying along the road in Godzone. It appeared in front of the man, drawing itself up to its full height, roaring and screaming, and vomiting green slime like it had seen in the movies. The man simply raised his hat and kept walking. Perplexed, the demon flew a little further along the road. This time it appeared as a huge spitting cobra, so large that it almost blocked the road. The man lifted his stick, whopped off the snake's head, and continued on his way.

The demon pulled itself together and determined to have one more try. It marshaled all its strength and took the form of a psychopathic ax murderer, complete with severed head in one hand.

As the man approached, the demon waved the double-edged ax in slow circles above its head. The man looked up, smiled, and waved back. The astonished demon fell in beside the man.

"Tell me traveler," it said, "why are you not afraid!"

"Oh but I am," replied the man. "I'm afraid that if my heart keeps producing this sort of rubbish I won't reach my destination before sundown."

Fear is an effective way of controlling people. It is used for fencing bad religion. By flooding the imagination, it drives out the capacity for love and so for God. Who can love when they cannot trust? But those who are afraid come running to priests and wizards, looking for the shelter of a rigid authority. The price they pay for it is their freedom. They condemn themselves to the prison of security, all the time having their fears fed by the keepers. To borrow a phrase from an innkeeper of the Zone, "Fear clouds their eyes like mental rheumatism."

"Perfect love," said Jesus, "drives out fear." The antidote to fear is a healthy bulking of the love of God. In its safety the twisted and tormented soul can unwind and learn to see clearly again. As trust and faith grow, the timid travelers can find their feet and head back to the road. The further they travel, the more fears they face and conquer, the deeper is the knowledge that while American Express may fail, there is nothing anywhere that can separate them from the love of God.

The Six-Lane Highway

The fastest way to get somewhere is not always the best. A hitchhiker in a hurry may be tempted to take the highway. It is certainly quicker, but like a kiss through a train window, it leaves a lot to be desired. The great highways bypass towns and tunnel through mountains. They teach nothing of the country they stream across. They allow no encounter with the local people or culture; you have to read the signs to know where you are. In any case, hitchhikers are generally banned from the highways as a traffic hazard.

The path through Godzone can often be steep and hard. When road-weary pilgrims come to a crossroads and discover a six-lane highway heading to their destination, they may succumb to the promise of a shortcut. The apparent easy road often leads the unsuspecting traveler out of the Zone again, or else keeps circling back on itself. These sealed highways are dangerous to seekers after the heartland, the more so because they tend to crop up at the most arduous points of the journey. You may flop down at the crossroads and discover an air conditioned coach pulled up at a picnic area for lunch. The tourists are fat and happy and share their chicken legs and salmon sandwiches with you. They worry about you, and tell stories they have heard about the bandits in the back country to which you are headed. It just so happens that they have a spare seat in the bus, and the highway they travel will eventually get you where you want to go. Hey, they're travelers too; this particular party is on a tour of the Holy Lands. Come on board, be kind to yourself for once.

It's hard to shoulder your pack and head off uphill again. But you can be sure that the narrow rutted track is yours. No one said Godzone was easy. It's difficult to leave behind the luxury lanes when you're tired and lonely. Console yourself that the fast tracks don't lead in your direction, despite what the signs may say. The donkey trail you follow may seem even less promising than a New Age revival meeting, but by sticking to it you will get a little further along in your journey.

If you do happen to surrender in a moment of weakness, and wake to find yourself staring out the tinted windows as the asphalt flashes by, don't worry. Stop the bus, get off, and find your way to the nearest rutted track that crosses the highway. You will have been side-tracked as surely as a teacher on a tangent, but the journey can begin again. Nothing is lost save a little pride and inexperience. It may be that you needed that diversion to realize just how tired you had got. A time of rest will bring your strength back, and allow you to laugh at yourself for being so dumb.

Guilt Swamp

Swamps suck. No bog is stickier for pilgrims of the Zone than that of guilt. The trouble starts with a moral mishap. You do something you didn't mean to—tell a lie, hurt someone, be selfish, ignore a cry for help. It makes you feel bad, guilty. The last person you want to talk to is your Lover. So you avoid God, as much as that's possible. Inside you feel soiled and stained. You don't like yourself for what you've done. And on top of that you begin to think, "God won't want to see me now." Already your feet have begun to sink.

So what do you do? Like a self-centered sadist, you punish yourself. You overeat or get drunk or sleep with a stranger or belt the kids. That makes you feel good and bad. But you are now guilty as hell, convinced that you have wandered outside the circle of God's love. You begin to hate yourself and set out to punish yourself some more. That helps to increase the weight on your back, and you sink deeper and deeper into the swamp of guilt. If the cycle isn't broken, you'll be lost without trace.

Mercifully, there is a way back to solid ground. That's to rediscover the love of God. It is perhaps not surprising that God should see and understand your secret failings; what takes time to get used to is the forgiveness that goes with it. If your guilt leads you gently back to the mercy of God, it has done well. If it draws you away, it is sick. Healing comes only through learning again that you are totally and completely accepted, that your stumbling and straying is no more resented than a child's curiosity. God will pick you up, dust you off, and put you back on the road.

Wanderers in the heartland are as great a bunch of bumbleheads as you have ever seen, but they know where to go when they're hurting. Through painful experience they have got in the habit of not carrying burdens around with them.

An old and a young monk, on their way to the monastery, came across a very beautiful woman at the river bank. Like them, she wanted to cross the river, but the water was too high. The older monk lifted her up onto his shoulders and waded across to the other side. The young monk was scandalized. All the way back to the monastery he fumed inwardly. Did his older brother not know that it was forbidden for a monk to have contact with a woman? What would people think of the Order if they saw such a disgraceful action?

Finally, he could stand it no longer and began to lecture his companion on the errors of his ways. The old monk listened until the tirade was finished. Then he said quietly, "Brother, I dropped that woman at the river. Are you carrying her still?"

You get no pixie points for carrying more weight than is necessary. The average punter makes enough mistakes in each day to suffice; there is no need to be crushed by the shortcomings of a whole life. The ongoing joy of life in Godzone is a continuing fresh start, looking to the road ahead and forgetting what has gone before. You may cling to your faults if you wish; wallow in the quagmire of guilt like a pig in a poo-pond. It is your choice. But God has forgotten and is more interested in the road ahead than agonized post-mortems of your misadventures.

Here is a fable from the Zone, slightly censored. A barefooted old man points a finger at the sky and breaks wind. The young and puritanical woman who accompanies him is shocked.

"I just shot an angel," he says.

She does not laugh.

"Do you know why I do that?" he asks. "Knocking off the angels makes room for a few more humans in heaven."

"You're a terrible old man," she says. But the man does not mind.

"Do you know what the angels do when I shoot them!" he grins. "They go to God and they say, 'That man down there is shooting our tail-feathers off.' And what do you think God says? He says, 'Shove off! I've given that man his freedom.'"

Hard Hearts

Callused hands may be an indication of an honest laborer. It is a natural process (the callusing), a means of protecting the hands from the effects of abrasion. Hearts get callused too, though for different reasons. If your private sorrow leads you away from God instead of drawing you closer, the walls of your heart thicken in defense. From the outside, your heart will be tough as barbecued goat—so tough that you take pride in it. On the inside you are bleeding. But who can ever see the inside?

It is difficult to irrigate hard ground. The water slides off the dry surface. The only way to make baked earth productive again is to put the plow through it, to break it up. It is preferable, however, to your life becoming barren and sour, unable to support life. The danger for Godzoners is that they may react to suffering by becoming bitter. When hard times come, as they inevitably do in the Zone, some leatherheads try to stay staunch and resist the process. They succeed only in incubating their pain.

Concrete is protective but not attractive. You can seal your heart tighter than the privy in a fallout shelter, but it gets awfully close in there after a while. How can God speak through a lead door? The thorny nut of cynicism gives little comfort in the long safe nights. Perhaps the hardest part of being tough is the loneliness. How can you express the longing and aching without blowing your cover? There is meager satisfaction in building secure castles on the rocky crags of Godzone; no one will pass by.

Enemies

Enemies are people who try to do you down. Hitchhikers are familiar with the rednecks who drive straight for them, or who stop fifty meters up the road, wait till the weary hiker has sprinted to the car, and then drive off. Whoever takes to the roads of Godzone had better be prepared for enemies. The very existence of the Zone arouses the wrath of the power-wielders, and those who travel its paths are as cherished as wowsers in a winery. Over the years they have been beaten, tortured, mocked, imprisoned, and executed. To suffer at the hands of your enemies is nothing more than par for those who caddy for Jesus.

It is common knowledge what you do with enemies; you hate them. You fight them with all your energy, doing unto them before they do unto you. Jesus was of a different opinion. "Love your enemies," he said, "and pray for those who persecute you." This comes as naturally to people as swimming to a cat. It is an inhuman expectation, if only because it is the sort of love that God has. But there it is, and Jesus, who was undoubtedly one of us, achieved it as his enemies crucified him.

If enemies pose a danger to Godzoners, it is the danger that they may draw the pilgrim into their own web of hatred. To return hate is to multiply it; to meet it with love is make it as powerless as an alligator with lockjaw. Whoever refuses to retaliate against violence to themselves exposes the aggressors for what they are. It is difficult to keep kicking a person who offers no resistance. Unfortunately, this does not stop violent people from overcoming the difficulty, but it does bring their hatred into the open. Jesus suggested turning the other cheek. He might just as well have said, "If they nail one hand to the cross, offer them the other one also."

This is not a training program for wimps. There is no point in someone refraining from retaliation unless they have some other choice. People such as Gandhi and Martin Luther King were no marshmallows. It takes courage and strength of spirit not to be engulfed by hatred. Those who possess it overcome their enemies, even though it often costs them life. It is the strategy taken by God, who defeats evil, not through meeting it head-on like a bison at a brick wall, but by absorbing its hatred, redeeming it through suffering.

No pioneer can afford to be naive about enemies. As with kids, learning to love them entails recognizing their existence.

And part of such love may require opposing the violence they do to the innocent. God does not require you to throw yourself in front of every passing train. Jesus read the signs and knew when the day had come for him to enter Jerusalem. He chose the time and place; he retained the initiative. Nonviolence is an active program for the self-destruction of evil. It needs to travel with its eyes open.

A dog approached the river bank, and found a scorpion stranded there. The dog cowered, aware of the lethal sting in the tail of this traditional enemy.

"Don't be afraid," said the scorpion to the dog. "I am stuck here on this side of the river and need to get across. Will you let me climb on your back while you swim?" it asked.

"No way," replied the dog. "If I do, you will sting me halfway across and I will drown."

"That would be stupid," said the scorpion. "Then I would perish as well." The dog was very reluctant, but eventually with the faithful promise to refrain from stinging allowed the scorpion to climb on its back. Halfway across, the scorpion embedded its sting in the dog's back.

"Why did you do that?" asked the dog before it died.

"It's in my nature to sting," replied the drowning scorpion.

Self-Deceit

An ancient Chinese proverb: "Those who swim in sewage find it hard to see the bottom." Humans are notorious for deceiving themselves. Self-deception is the most common and most damaging form of lying. We build our images and then try to live up to them, watching ourselves in shop windows to see how we're going. We pretend to be sensitive while looking for an inside chance to manipulate others. We rename things to make ourselves innocent. "Wrong" becomes "inappropriate"; "exploitation" becomes "revenue earning"; "selfishness" becomes "assertive self-reinforcement." But crap by any other name still has a distinctive smell.

There are none so blind as those who will not see. And self-deception is a certain route to blindness. Godzoners are not immune from human foibles. It is possible for travelers to give up the journey but still collect pennants from souvenir shops to fool themselves that they are heading somewhere. Sojourners can get into self-destructive habits, assuring themselves that they're just exploring the full range of experience. Others block their eyes and ears, go into hiding from God and the world, and call it self-discovery. "When the blind lead the blind," said Jesus, "both fall into the ditch."

It is subtle, this danger. To every pusher's profit, attractive fantasy is easier to accept than an unpleasant reality. Who wants to face their inner darkness? Simpler by far to wallpaper over the crevasse and bolt the door of the cellar. That way everything can stay nice, and no one need know that the ceiling is false. There appears to be no limit to the capacity of the human heart to fool itself. "The Emperor's New Clothes" is more than a story for children. Self-deception must steer well clear of anything resembling a mirror.

An oriental king married off his ugly daughter to a blind man, because no one else would have her. When a doctor offered to restore the blind man's sight, the father of the girl would not allow it. He was afraid that if the man once saw his daughter, he would divorce her.

Not everyone wants their cataracts removed, for the same reason that communist czars kept their luxury discreet; exposure is not always in their interest. Light hurts the eyes when it is seen for the first time, and truth is painful before it is liberating. Nevertheless, no one can travel the Zone with their eyes clouded. The crap must be washed away so that the road ahead can be clearly seen.

God is regarded as an enemy by the dim-sighted dung-beetles who push their illusions busily uphill. They are scared to let go of that which they have created, even if it is made of dung.

A man went into a store with a sign outside which read "The Truth Shop." The woman behind the counter was very polite. What type of truth did the gentleman wish to purchase; partial or whole?

"The whole truth, of course," said the man. "No deceptions for me, no defenses, no rationalizations. I want my truth plain and unadulterated." The woman waved him to the other side of the store. There a salesman at the desk pointed to the price tag.

"The price is very high, sir," he said. "Are you sure you can afford it?"

"What is it?" asked the man. He was determined to get the whole truth, no matter what it cost.

"Your security, sir," replied the salesman. The man walked away with a heavy heart. He was not yet ready to be bankrupted for the sake of truth.

The dangers of Godzone, though they be as pervasive as pimples, are all overcome through the simple ruse of staying in close contract with your Quiet Companion. Every imaginable situation has been faced and conquered by pilgrims with faithful hearts. They know that whatever happens, God is close at hand. A few thousand years ago, a traveler who had survived a few scrapes sat down to pen a song. Here's how it goes:

Where can I go from your Spirit?
Where can I flee from your presence?
If I soar through heaven, you are there!
If I make my bed in hell, you are there!
If I take the wings of the morning
And fly to the uttermost stretch of the sea,
Even there your right hand leads me and holds me.
If I say, "let darkness cover me as a cloak,
And the light about me be as night,"
Even the darkness is not dark to you;
The night is as bright as the day,
For darkness is as light to you.

6

TRAVELING COMPANIONS

There is an old hitchhiker's ruse, probably first tried on Noah by wet and worried nonswimmers. An unsuspecting motorist pulls over for a lone curvaceous backpacker with her thumb out. As he opens the boot to throw in her scant luggage, out from the bushes at the side of the road emerges her hairy male friend, carrying two large suitcases and a guitar, and with a flea-bitten mongrel at his heels. He quickly occupies the front seat, puts the goat-rank dog on his lap, and asks cheerfully, "How far are you going?" It's a dirty trick, but it gets rides when there's more than one of you traveling together.

For most of us, the road is company enough. It keeps confidences and tells no lies. But asphalt is hard to snuggle up to at night. Even the most travel-creased and staunch traveler craves friendship, someone to be intimate with. Generally the rides we catch don't fit the bill. They are measured in miles, and you don't want to leave too much behind in a car you have to get out of. A defensive game for hitchhikers is "Who shall I be?" The idea is to choose a different identity for every ride, and flesh it out in response to the inevitable question "Where are you from?" It's fun while it lasts, but you run the danger of forgetting which story is the real one.

Intimacy tends to be reserved for people sharing your addiction to the road—either fellow pilgrims or those you meet around a winter's fire on overnight stops. When it comes, it is as surprising as a cheerful undertaker, as uninvited as a skeptic at a spoonbenders' conference. Travelers learn to receive it gladly, to take what is offered and refrain from grasping. They live in the knowledge that come morning the road leads on. Maybe there will be another meeting further down the road, maybe not. For the moment there are jokes and stories, freedom to be yourself with someone who understands, the fun of sharing humanity, if not sleeping bags.

Travelers of Godzone also find companions of the Way. They share the road with fellow drifters and desperados. These weird and woolly wanderers are gifts from God to you. They do not always appear that way at first. Sometimes they seem as useful as the silver serviette ring that Aunt Agnes sends to you care of Poste Restante. But when the time comes to part, you realize that this chance meeting was the right person at the right time and that your life is all the fuller and richer for the meeting. We need these little reminders that we don't travel alone, and that Godzone existed before we ever started to explore it.

The Soloist Syndrome

Soloists are good in small doses and dull in endurance. They are best of all when their performance floats out above a foundation laid by other instruments, hovers and dances, and then drifts back into the progression. Universally, soloists get to like their own sound. They always want to be a little louder for a little longer. Eventually they decide they can do very well without the need of backing. This dismissal of the long-suffering musos who have carried them is all too simple. It paves the way to busking in back streets.

Godzone has its fair share of gun-toting lone rangers and spiritual soloists. They keep themselves to themselves and ride off into the setting sun with romantic disregard for anyone else. It's "God and me" all the way, and the devil take the hindmost. Unfortunately for these carefree cowboys, they are the ones taken. Their rugged independence lasts at least until the first crisis, at which point solitude loses its attraction. Those called to travel the Zone find themselves part of a great company of sojourners, to be ignored only at one's peril.

A *very* spiritual man named John shared a house with his older brother. One day he came to his brother and said, "I want to be free from worldly cares; I find that working and talking distract me from worshipping God." He bade goodbye to his brother, changed out of his working clothes, and headed off into the desert to be alone.

One week later, John returned to his brother's house, and knocked at the door. His brother did not open it, but called from inside.

"Who is it?"

"It's John, your brother," came the reply.

"Oh no," said the brother, "John has become an angel and needs neither food nor company anymore."

John knocked and begged, crying "It's me!"

But his brother left him sitting there all through the night.

When he finally opened the door the next morning, John hugged him.

It is easy to be pious in your own company. Humility requires the image supplied by the mirrors in the eyes of friends. God has called us to community, a new way of being in which we recognize our belonging to and need for each other. Every survivor in the Zone learns to reach out and grasp another's hand at points along the way. Sometimes it is to help, sometimes to be helped, sometimes simply for the reassurance of skin on skin. The seeming self-containment of loners turns out to be no substitute for the real thing.

Friends Along the Way

None of us invented God. And the roads of Godzone, new though they may be to us, are in fact well traveled. There are many friends to lead us through the narrow passes. Some of them are here to walk beside us; others have left behind their scribblings and fragments for us to use if we choose. As Stanley said to Livingstone, time spent in reconnaissance is seldom wasted. Newcomers are full of opinions and shortcuts; like small children, they have to fall a few times before they believe that gravity affects them as well. God sends us guides and companions to help us keep our feet on the path.

Like the one Hollywood plot, they come in many different guises. It is possible to not recognize them, or even to regard them as enemies at first. They have these things in common: they know God, they know the Zone, and they are travelers themselves. They are the sort of people who will pass on a book for you to read, ask you questions that make you angry, or hang around for you outside the police station with a thermos and a bag of sandwiches. They will share their pointed jokes, their bottle of wine, and most importantly, their knowledge of the road. They come and they go, leaving you grateful and a little sad, but always stronger.

A few will become as familiar as the sound of your own breathing. Friends you meet with at irregular intervals and in unlikely places, discovering again and again that your wanderings, while separate, have kept pace with each other. These are the ones in whose presence you are as relaxed as a basset-hound on barbiturates. Mates you can abuse and be your silly self with, knowing that they will still be there in the morning. And then in the quiet times, strolling down an empty road in the twilight peace, you trade words that are so precious and fragile you fear they will shatter on the air.

Your journey is a thread. It weaves backwards and forwards, falters, ducks and dives, always wending its way onwards and upwards. On its own it makes as much sense as the trail of a glue-sniffing crab. But your journey is never on its own, whether you see it or not. It interlocks with other threads of other travelers and becomes woven into the unfolding fabric. Friends along the way are the stitches that lock you into the design. Sometimes as you look back, you catch glimpses of a bright tapestry. But it will take a much greater distance to be able to see entirely the pattern of the weave.

Companions often change your direction. Never by manipulation or moralizing, but by the sincerity of their friendship and the wisdom of their words. It is only some distance along the way, after you have taken the risk of trusting, that your friend will speak the magic sentence that opens your eyes to a new signpost, a fresh calling from the Lover within. It is grace; it never loses its ability to astonish. Your friend may leave shortly after offering that gift, not to be seen again this side of the fiver. But the gift remains, and the sign of thanksgiving is to use it.

Making room for friends gives space for God. The story is told of young Francis of Assisi, out riding on the great open plains below the town. A wealthy young man, he was trialing his father's newest horse. The speed and the freedom were exhilarating. Off in the distance he saw a small dot, which quickly formed into a man as he approached. Francis reined in his mount to greet this traveler who was trudging along exposed in the noon sun. It was only as he stopped in front of the hunched figure that he realized it was a leper.

The sight and the smell were appalling. As the pathetic creature reached out its claw-like hand to beg, Francis felt a wave of nausea rise within him. His sheltered upbringing had protected him from facing the bearers of this dreaded disease. As he was about to flee, a strange thing happened. Francis envisaged the leper with his own face. He was struck with compassion, and leapt down from the horse. Without taking time to think, he embraced the man and kissed the festered lips. He reached into the folds of his robe and produced a small purse of gold pieces for the leper. Mounting again, he rode off a few paces and turned back. For as far as the eye could see, the plain was empty.

Campsites

One thing gypsies do better than most is traveling. The heart of their journeying together is the celebration around the fire at stops along the way. When the flames leap and the violins and guitars come out, the people dance. There they remember the truth of who they are, recall the places they have been together, and find in each other inspiration to go on. Gypsies without such celebrations would not be gypsies.

Godzoners need their times of celebration as well—times when they meet with other travelers at the side of the road to rejoice in the Zone and its Maker, times to sing and dance and tell stories long into the night. Where they meet, the world rolls back and the Zone is established on earth. The simple act of gathering transforms everything. As with an orchestra, the whole that is created is greater than the sum of the individual parts that form it. Each traveler brings something of God, and the combination somehow draws God out of the shadows and into the light.

It is this need for the wayfarers to gather that brought churches into existence. "Church" at one time meant a gathering of people. Now it means a building with a steeple. "Worship" at one time meant the act of celebrating God's presence. Now it means a collection of rituals at 11 A.M. on a Sunday morning. "Faith" at one time was a red-blooded response to the stirring of the Spirit. Now it is a set of beliefs so insignificant that they can be contained in doctrines. The Way has become religion, its meaning drowned in a sea of ceremony.

How does this happen? There was once a teacher of great faith and insight. Several disciples gathered around him to learn from his wisdom. It so happened that each time the small community met for prayer, the cat would come in and distract them. The teacher ordered the cat tied whenever the community prayed. Eventually the great one died, but the cat continued to be tied up at worship time. When the cat died, another cat was bought to make sure that the teacher's wishes were still faithfully observed. Centuries passed, and learned treatises were written by scholarly disciples on the liturgical significance of tying up a cat while worship is performed.

There is no doubt that such disciples are mistaken. But the answer is not to kill the cat, nor to imagine that prayer or worship are unimportant. Too many modern churches resemble museums full of relics rather than vibrant communities of adventurers. Often the rites are empty, the music leaden, the lips tight and unyielding. Nevertheless, beneath that dry and crusty shell, there are pearls of truth still to be recovered. Drifters avoid churches unless the door is unlocked and it's raining outside. But travelers of the Zone cannot for long avoid the hunger to get together and worship.

Worship is greatly misunderstood. God is not some egomaniac who needs constant affirmation, some sort of neurotic narcissist. Those who set out to buy God off with the sacrifice of the odd Sunday morning sleep-in could not be further from the truth. Worship is for those who have been run down by the Hound of heaven. For these whose hearts have been shafted with love, worship is as natural and as unavoidable as a tree coming into blossom with the warmth of spring. It is love language, no more accessible to nonparticipants than the words that pass across the pillow between two lovers.

To hold worship back would be as difficult for a Wayfarer as silence for a child making a new discovery. It has to be expressed, and in its expression comes honesty and reality. The truth about we humans is that we have been made from love, and it is only in love that we discover what we are. Worship releases us, like caged birds returned to the air, into our natural environment, and we discover that we can swoop and soar and dive. The forms it takes are as manifold as potential aerial maneuvers, but they lead us to God and so to freedom. "You worship what you know," said Jesus to a woman theologian. "But the time has come to worship in spirit and in truth."

Like many other activities, worship is best experienced in company. The more people the deeper it gets. Strange things sometimes happen, but these are best not talked about. Suffice it to say that when Zone-travelers congregate, nothing remains the same. Worship must always spring from the road and lead back onto it. Nothing gets up God's nose more than the pretense of worship by shiny-bummed pew-sitters who have yet to begin the journey. Except perhaps those who use the name of God while degrading people. They live dangerously, because their so-called worship is blasphemy, and God sees.

For those who express their Godlove in the way they live, however, worship brings the journey into focus. There is the looking back to see the distance already covered, the songs that recall the mountains and the valleys. There is the looking ahead, the dreaming and wondering and encouraging one another toward the horizon. And there is the present and the Presence, the awesome all-consuming reality of God among us, wooing and healing and creating. In the womb of this community of worship, all things become new.

Sharing the Bread

On the night before Jesus was arrested by the State, he was feasting with his friends and fellow-travelers. Having a strong intuition about what was coming, he wanted to leave them something to think about. So he took the bread that was on the table and broke it before passing it around, telling them that his body would also be broken and shared. Then he filled the cup with wine and sent that around as well, saying that his life would be poured out for all. "Whenever you do this," said Jesus, "remember me."

From that time on, pilgrims of the heart have paused at points along the Way, broken a loaf of bread and shared a cup of wine, and remembered Jesus who died but never dies. Often it is more than just memory; travelers have been heard to swear that there was an extra person at the table, and that his hands seemed scarred.

But for those who travel the roads and share their tables with rogues and nutters, the breaking of bread carries forward the life of one who sat down with all. Coffee and chocolate cake can do it instead of bread and wine—whatever is at hand. In the breaking and the emptying, the sharing and the friendship, there is an acting out of what the journey is all about. All common things become sacred, and God is as near at hand as the food on the table. Soon every meal becomes an acted-out parable of God's love made real in Jesus, every guest a sister or brother.

Storytelling

When travelers come together, they tell stories—stories about the road, stories about people, stories about themselves, stories about God. No one should doubt the power of stories. An old man who had been paralyzed for many years was asked to tell a story about his former teacher. He started off on a tale of how the holy man used to jump up and down and dance when he was praying. While he was telling the story, the old man stood up; the story carried him away so much that he too had to jump and dance to show how the master had done it. From that moment he was healed.

Stories are a way of sharing truth without lecturing or moralizing. The listener chooses his or her own level of involvement and draws as much or as little meaning as desired. But it is almost impossible to stay on the outside of a story. It is said of the Greek orator Demades that he once had difficulty capturing the attention of his audience. They laughed and talked among themselves, looked up into the sky, and generally displayed their lack of interest.

So Demades began, "Ceres one day journeyed in company with a swallow and an eel." At this there was a sudden attention, and every ear strained to catch the words of the orator.

When the Domeheads and Footnote-readers asked Jesus "Who is my neighbor," they were looking for a three-point technical definition that could be perused for error. Instead, he told them a story about a Samaritan on his way to Jericho. They were drawn into the tale like wasps to a picnic, and so felt its sting even more when it came. Jesus was a great storyteller. One of the reasons he was crucified was because his stories cut right to the bone. They stripped away the piety and pretension, leaving the crowd naked before the truth.

When two Zone-combers trade tales across a table, they sometimes tell their own stories, and leave in the bad bits. By speaking their doubts and fears, their disappointments and failures, they are purged as thoroughly as an emetic empties a stomach. To bring out the worst from the dark inner caverns is to take away the power of it. Telling your story to a person worthy of trust, you hear it for the first time yourself. You sense the magic, see the deft hand of God at work, recognize the needless pain of having kept secrets. The grace by which you are healed extends to the listener, building a bridge between you over which love passes.

God is the original storyteller, life an uncompleted novel, with the author yet to reveal the outcome of the plot. When the sparks drift and tongues loosen in the night, God is both listener and yarn-spinner. God has a long memory, stretching way back to before the world or the Zone came into being. Out of it flow the tales that clear the fog and light the way.

David was a man of passion. The same fervor with which he loved God often got him into trouble. But being king of Israel meant he could usually get himself out of it again. One day when he was sunbathing on the roof of the palace, something caught his eye. On the roof of a house below him (all the other roofs were lower, naturally), he saw a woman slowly undress and step into a bath. She was an olive beauty, and David's resolution, among other things, grew hard. Though he knew she was married, he invited Bathsheba (for that was her name) up to his room to see his regalia. They spent an abandoned night together before she returned to her home. Shortly afterwards David was informed that she had admitted royalty to her chamber; she was pregnant. What made this particularly difficult was that her husband was away with the troops fighting a war. David attempted to cover his tracks by ordering that Bathsheba's husband, Uriah, be sent home for a bit of R & R. Surely he would make love in preference to war, and thus provide an alibi for the untimely conception. Unfortunately, Uriah, though poor, was a man of great principle. He gallantly refused to sleep with his wife while his fellow soldiers were slogging it out on the battlefield. So David ordered Uriah sent into the front line and left in a suicidal position, where he was conveniently killed by the enemy.

David was pleased that the lid was placed on his own 'Jerusalemgate," and rewarded himself by adding the widow Bathsheba to his already substantial collection of wives. One day a filthy old prophet named Nathan came staggering down from the hills and demanded an audience with the king. He proceeded to tell David a story.

"Once there were two farmers," he said. "One was rich and had hundreds of sheep, and the other was a poor man with nothing but one little ewe lamb. It grew up with the children, they knew it by name, and the lamb became as a daughter to the poor man. One day the rich farmer had to entertain a guest. But he didn't want to lose any of his great herd of sheep, so instead he stole the poor man's lamb, killed it, and served it up to the guest."

As David listened, he was filled with righteous anger. He rose to his feet and declared, "By God, the man who did this despicable thing deserves to die."

Nathan fixed David with a look he would never forget, and said quietly, "You are the man."

There is no sillier question than that as to whether a story is true or not. If a story is heard, it leads to truth; if not, it is an empty tale. The listener is the one who decides, and so the answer to the question lies with the asker. One thing is sure. The wisdom of the Zone is passed by story, and good stories, like fleas and cockroaches, never die. Wherever Godzoners gather, the legends will be told and the old magic begin to work.

Dingbats and Deadheads

Generally, friends are people you feel some affinity for. It's no effort to relate to them. But to enter the Zone is to become part of a weird family of travelers. Many of them will seem to you to display ingrained dingbat qualities, worthy of contempt. Beware! These are the ones who have the most to teach you. To accept such geeky deadheads as brothers and sisters of the Way will flatten the shell of your pride like a snail beneath a steamroller. It does you no harm to learn that God doesn't love you for your good looks or fine taste. If you can make it on the road, how can God be choosy? The wisdom of the Zone is that differences add flavor, variety, and color, and angular souls pungency and love.

In the world relationships are built on common interests. In Godzone the only basis is belonging, and so the traveler has to accept all whom God accepts. It's sometimes easier to love God than to love God's mates. The problem is that you can't do one without the other.

The claim to love has to be tested against the reality of people with body odor and strange habits, if it is to be any more than a warm gooey feeling. This road we follow is a journey into community. If we are to reach the final destination we must learn to see the God-light in the most unlikely of characters. We must discover that differences are enriching rather than threatening. This only comes after the hard nut of self has been cracked.

There was once an old monastery that had lost its inspiration. The same routines were performed as they always had been, but there were no new novices and little enthusiasm for the rites of prayer.

The abbot saw all this and grieved. At a loss as to how to change things, he paid a visit to an old hermit who lived deep in the woods. The hermit welcomed him and spread the table with bread and cheese and wine. After they had eaten together, the recluse addressed the abbot.

"You and your brothers have lost the fire of God. You come seeking wisdom from me. I will tell you a secret, but you can only repeat it once. After that, no one must say it aloud again."

The hermit then looked deep into the eyes of the abbot and said, "The Messiah is among you."

They were both silent as the abbot considered the import of this saying. "Now you must leave," the hermit said.

Returning to the monastery, the abbot called all the monks together and told them that he had a teaching that had been given by God. He added that the teaching was never to be repeated out loud again. Then the abbot looked at each of his brothers, and said, "The hermit says that one of us is the Messiah."

The monks were startled. "What could it mean?" they wondered silently. "Is John with the big nose the Messiah? Or Father Matthew who falls asleep at prayer? Am I the Messiah?" But puzzled as they were, they never repeated the saying again.

As time went by, the monks began to treat one another with a special love and reverence. There was a gentle, wholehearted, human quality about them now that was hard to describe but easy to see. They lived with each other as those who had finally found something of significance. Their words were carefully considered and gentle. Who could tell when they might be speaking to the Messiah?

Before long, the vitality of the monastery attracted many visitors and young men began asking to join the community. The old hermit died without revealing any more, and the abbot sometimes wondered if he had understood correctly.

God has given us each other so that we may learn the truth about ourselves. When you run head on into a real turkey, guess who needs plucking? When the feathers of our vanity are finally shed, love and acceptance do not seem as difficult as they once were. A man once said he would believe in God only when he could be taught all that was necessary while standing on one foot. He was dismissed by many priests as being disrespectful. Finally he found one who offered to do it.

"Love God, and show it by loving your neighbor as yourself," said the canny priest. "All the rest is decoration."

Loving our friends as we love ourselves takes long enough. Loving our neighbors in that way takes the whole of the journey. But we none of us travel alone, and the adventure will not be finished until every one of us has made it to the end. Our companions on the Way are not only sharing the road, they are a part of it. Even the dingbats. Even you.

7

THE LAST FRONTIER

Flat-earthers have this to their credit: they picture the world as having an edge. The rest of us, geographically correct as we might be, are condemned to round trips. This inability to get off can be confining; a world without end provides only a limited sphere of discovery. No explorer likes to feel trapped or limited by geographical circumstances. Without a beyond, life quickly grows as dreary as a political speech on a wet afternoon, and almost as empty of meaning. No wonder Albert Camus got depressed.

It is on the edges of the world that Godzone begins. That's why it is more easily found by those on the fringes of society. Godzone is far out, even though it's always right at hand. The further you get from the center of the world, the nearer to the Zone. In this frontier land, however, the edges are not sharp. The two realms merge with each other. Like severe ghosting on a television set, it's difficult to tell which is the real image. They are overlapping, yet distinct. It is only when the tuning is correct that one will fade and other become clear.

A Mr. Nicholas Scotti once made a trip from America to visit relatives in his native Italy. When the plane stopped to refuel at Kennedy airport, Mr. Scotti got out and spent two days in New York, believing himself to be in Rome. His relatives were not there to meet him, but he generously assumed that they had been held up in the heavy Roman traffic. While trying to locate them, the surprised traveler noticed that most of the great city's landmarks had been laid waste by progress. He also couldn't help wondering at the number of people who were obviously American, but put it down to the great wave of tourism. He further assumed that so many signs were in English for the benefit of these tourists.

He finally found a police officer, and asked him in Italian the way to the bus station. It so happened that the officer came from Naples, and replied fluently in Mr. Scotti's native tongue. When he could not be dislodged from the bus, the bus driver handed over the puzzled sightseer to another police officer. A fierce argument resulted, with Mr. Scotti scarcely believing that the Rome police force would employ someone who did not speak Italian. Even when assured he was in New York, Scotti refused to believe it. The police raced him to the airport with sirens screaming to put him on a plane back to San Francisco. "See," said Scotti to his interpreter, "I know I'm in Italy. That's how they drive!"

Those who have not been reborn can't see the Zone, and they won't believe in it, though their toes are tickled by an angel. Those who travel the Zone live in both realms and speak two languages. They are in the world but not of the world. They belong to Godzone but breathe the same air as everyone else. In this no-man's land between already and not yet, God is making one into the other. The Zone is essentially subversive, its pilgrims fifth columnists who dance to the beat of a drum that few can hear.

But there comes a point where the double life ends, as Monica Lewinsky can testify. Godzoners are uncomfortable in the world; they itch with a longing for the heartland. "All God's chillun get weary, Lord," as the old sojourners' song has it, "Don't it make you want to go home?" It does, but on the utmost border of the world is a river few are eager to cross. It marks the end of the road, and it is so wide and deep the other side is indistinct and mysterious. To wade into it is to let go of every secure footing. The name of the river is Death.

The Last Laugh

A burly farmer was impressed with the advertising for a chainsaw. "Guaranteed to cut two cords of timber in an hour" read the sign. He bought one and took it home with eager anticipation. The next day he was back in the shop.

"This saw is no good," he said to the shop assistant. "I could only get through a little under one cord in an hour— and even then I was working hard."

The assistant was very apologetic and replaced the chainsaw with a new one. But the next day the farmer was back again. "No good," he said. " Just over a cord this time." The assistant was more puzzled than ever. He examined the saw in minute detail, and eventually started it up. The farmer jumped back several paces in fright.

"What's that noise?" he asked.

What makes a joke? It is a story with a twist in its tail that makes you laugh. You are carried along seeing things from one point of view, when one line causes you to see something unexpected and funny.

Mrs. Moskowitz was having her house painted, and between the smell of the paint and the hassle, she found life hard. It was the last straw when Mr. Moskowitz forgot himself and leaned against the wall, leaving a distinct hand mark on the fresh paint. His wife made her feelings known, while he tried to calm her.

"What's the fuss?" he said. "The painter's returning tomorrow, so he can just paint it over."

Nevertheless, Mrs. Moskowitz found it difficult to sleep all night. The thought of that hand mark bothered her. The next morning, the painter had barely stepped over the threshold when she was upon him saying, "Oh, I'm so glad you're here. All night long I've been thinking of you and waiting for you. Come with me. I want to show you where my husband put his hand." The painter blanched and stepped back aghast. "Please," he said, "I'm an old man. A cup of tea, and maybe some cake, is all I want!"

It is hopeless trying to explain a joke. If you once have to start, you know you've got a lame duck on your hands. You either get the joke or you don't. You see the twist and start laughing or you miss it altogether. Here is God's joke.

Jesus had one basic message. "Godzone is among you," he said, and he said it to the little people. The Bishops and Bonecrushers looked but could not see. They were not keen on any free entry scheme that might cut them out of their role as doorkeepers. The dark reptilian evil slithered up into their hearts from the mud and struck, dragging Jesus below the waters of death. There was much gloating in Slimytown. Fascists and Fearmongers celebrated their victory. It had all been so easy in the end. Jesus lay safely buried in a stone vault, his followers scattered, his dream hammered flat.

The third day began with a chuckle. The sun snickered as it climbed over the world's edge. The trees trembled and shook as they caught on. A great belly-laugh thundered from the earth to the sky, booming through the heavens. The tomb was empty; death was empty; hell was empty! Jesus was alive, alive with a life freshly immune to death. Every hammer blow on Golgotha had driven another nail into the coffin of the system. By the time the Life-leeches understood, it was too late. They themselves had planted the seed of love in the raw earth and now it had struck, never to be uprooted.

God had the last laugh. Often, as in the case of a karate instructor who wakes to hear intruders, the reversal of expectation has a certain satisfaction. At other times, the last laugh can be an empty victory.

A huge red-haired man came into a Derry pub and called out, "Would there be a man answering to the name of Murphy here?"

A thin lad stood up in the corner. "I'm Murphy," he said. "What can I be doing for you?"

The giant set upon him. He broke most of his ribs, knocked out two teeth, and shattered his nose. Then he strode out, leaving his victim flat out on the floor. Amazingly, the little guy started chuckling between his swollen lips.

"I sure fooled that fella," he wheezed. "I'm not Murphy at all!"

But God's laughter springs from the final turning of the tables. The worst of the world was aimed at God on that cross: evil, hatred, jealousy, fear, blasphemy, cruelty, revenge, death itself. It was all swallowed up in love as the sea absorbs a rainstorm, and changed, transformed into goodness and hope and unassailable life. Jesus did not just come alive again, like one of those birthday candles you can't blow out. He rose to a way of being that compares to human life as the sun to a torch. Jesus charted a way across the last frontier of Godzone. There, on the far bank, beyond further attack, he calls us to come over.

If you ask, "How?" you have missed the joke. Only people who like plastic flowers would indulge in the pedantry of explanation. But when you get it, you will find it hard to keep the smile off your face. Like a student who has just found an advance copy of the exam paper mailed to them by mistake, you will at times grin inappropriately. People may suspect either luck or lunacy. Some you may be able to share the joke with; others will get a glazed look as if you just told them about a new cure for baldness. God has a unique sense of humor; not everyone appreciates it.

Postcards From The Other Side

Postcards are the traveler's friend. They allow you to keep in touch without having to waste energy trying to remember what the news is. There's enough room to write, "Send more money," but not so much as to require three hours sucking a pen and looking into the distance. The pictures on the front always look romantic and exotic, belying the fact that you're holed up in a hovel shared with rats and cockroaches during the monsoon season. They're reassuring for the folks back home. Apart from anything else, postcards give posties something to read on their rounds.

When it comes to what lies on the other side of the last frontier, few are qualified to speak. Candidates either lack the experience or the means to communicate. The story is told of two monks who made a pact with each other. Whichever one died first would come back and tell the other what it was like. They worked out a code. One knock on the wall if everything was as they imagined it to be, two knocks if it was different, three if it was very different. The time came when one of them died, and the other waited expectantly in his cell for some communication. Late in the night there was a stirring and an eerie light in the room. The tapping began, and only ceased a great number of taps later when the monk cried out, "Stop! I get the message."

It is not for us to know in any depth what lies beyond the river. Those who try to steam open the envelope of death succeed only in burning their fingers. On the loony fringes there is a wide assortment of wizards, mediums, necromancers, and clairvoyants who will bring you words of comfort from the late Aunt Mary, but the only folk more gullible than they are their customers who pay for such fond deceptions. The idea that the dear departed have nothing better to do than answer silly questions directed to them through a spiritualist switchboard is depressing in the extreme.

Occasionally, however, Godzoners receive the equivalent of a postcard from the other side. It has no picture on the front nor message on the back. It is a hint, a feeling, an experience —a moment of insight such as comes to a scientist with a new synthesis. For a few enormous moments, you stand in a place where time has no meaning, and the air is heavy with the fragrance of God. It is a sneak preview of Life, a glimpse beyond the curtain, a taste from the pot before the meal begins. A gift it is, a promise of what is to come. And then it is gone, and there is no way of knowing whether it happened or not.

Often such postcards arrive when the road has become difficult. You're busted flat, the old toothache just started, your best friend is dying of cancer, it's raining, and you've got head lice. An old school friend who is now a television star just drove past in a BMW and splashed you. You feel like your whole journey is empty and without direction, as disappointing as an exercycle to a paraplegic. It is in this sucking bog of self-pity that the missive comes, sluicing through the despair and revealing a land of spectacular beauty. It is your inheritance, your destination, your homeland.

Of course, receiving a postcard is not the same as being there. It can be downright unsettling, like a cat rubbing your leg under the table at a restaurant. But it stirs weary Wayfarers into action, gives them new inspiration to keep on keeping on. It takes away the fear of the last river to be crossed as a steady hand might calm a young child. "In the meantime," wrote a great mapper of the Zone, "we see as if through smoky glass." But then, ah, then it shall be face to face.

The Greening of the World

A snake grows a new skin while still inside its old one. When the time comes, the withered old skin is sloughed off, and a new snake appears. It has been there all the time, of course; it was simply hidden beneath the surface. We are like that as well. When the time comes to lay down your old and friendly body, the person who has been growing quietly within steps out into the open. Death is as much a beginning as it is an end.

Coming to the top of a steep hill, Grasshopper found a large apple and decided to have lunch. He ate a big bite out of the side of it.

"Look what you did!" cried a worm who lived in the apple. "You've made a big hole in my roof. It's not polite to eat a person's house."

"I'm sorry," said Grasshopper. Just then the apple began to roll down the road on the other side of the hill.

"Stop me—Catch me!" cried the worm. The apple was rolling faster and faster. "Help, my head is bumping on the walls! My dishes are falling off the shelf!" cried the worm.

Grasshopper ran after the apple, but he couldn't catch it. It rolled all the way to the bottom of the hill, where it hit a tree and smashed into a hundred pieces.

"Too bad, worm," said Grasshopper. "Your house is gone." The worm climbed up the side of the tree.

"Oh, never mind," said the worm. "It was old, and it had a big bite out of it anyway. This is a fine time for me to find a new house."

Grasshopper looked up into the tree. He saw that it was filled with apples. Grasshopper smiled, and he went on down the road.

Losing everything familiar is not always such a bad thing. Apples rot, bodies decay, and even this old world comes to an end. It has, in fact, already come to an end. But Like a tired television soap, it doesn't know how to stop. Within the stretched and wrinkled skin of the world, the Zone grows. Soon it will become ripe and crack open the husk of the world as a fat green sprout splits the seed which spawned it. It can no more be contained than a small town can keep a secret or a bucket hold the wind. It is growing; silently, steadily, secretly growing.

We live between the ages, with each laying claim to our fealty. There are those who bind their lives to the dying system of the world and struggle to preserve it. There are those who, entering Godzone, set their sights on the far horizon and carve a wake of troubled waters through the world. There are those who religiously flirt with both realms, unsure which way to turn. The two orders clash and groan; the one in death throes, the other in the pangs of birth. The New Age is tearing the embryonic sac of history with its irrepressible surge of Life.

King Canute taught his followers a lesson: he was not God, and no way could he hold back the tide. Despite his royal edict, it kept on rolling in. The Zone is even now eddying around the foundations of the world, leeching away the sand they rest on. Many a castle will tumble in the ebb of the system. Godzone is here and now amongst us, and no petty bureaucrat or trickle-down monetarist will stem it. Whether you arrive at the last frontier of Godzone, or Godzone arrives at your front door, one way or the other the Zone will get you! You can no more avoid it than a fish can stay dry.

The Substance and the Shadow

Godzone is as real as a razor blade, and twice as sharp. To hedonists and loan sharks it seems ephemeral, as wispy and naive as a promise of fidelity or a money-back guarantee. From the clear air of the Zone, it is evident that quite the reverse is true. Godzone is the reality, the world bounded by convention and logic the pale illusion. In the pure light of God, the Clayton's existence that "realists" hold so dear is seen to be translucent and thin. It might at any moment evaporate like a morning mist, fade like a dream on the edge of wakefulness.

The peaks and valleys of the Zone, the customs and language that confound sensible living, the strange folk who haunt the roads in pursuit of God: these are the substance of reality. The rest is Shadowlands, a ghost town of egos and emptiness, full of nothing. Those who build their homes here scuttle across the skin of fantasy, puffed up with self-importance and pride, entranced by the trivial. They are oblivious to their own tragedy. Travelers of the Zone are blessed, and cursed, with the ability to see both the real world and its garbled reflection, and they long for the day of God to break. In that clear dawn the shadows will flee.

In the meantime, they inhabit the same space, and the Zone is a matter of perception. For those who have tasted once, nothing less than its hard reality will satisfy. God aches with the tragedy of this homeland scorned for the sake of a Butlin's holiday camp.

There was once a poor widow who lived in the city of Krakow. She dwelt with her four children on the street of the Lost Sheep, in a small basement apartment on the corner. Being so poor, she dreamed most nights of riches. One night she had an especially vivid dream. She dreamt that underneath a bridge in the city of Warsaw there was a great treasure. Waking the next morning, she could scarcely contain her excitement. She called her sister to look after the children, packed food and clothes, and set off on the long journey to find the bridge. After many days she arrived in Warsaw and found the place she sought. It was just as she had seen it in her dream, except for one thing. There was an armed guard on the bridge, who paced back and forward.

Tired from her journey, she collapsed among the bushes and fell asleep. She awoke much later, but as she rose, the guard spied her.

"You! Come here" said the guard.

Being a simple woman, she did not attempt to run.

"What are you doing here?" asked the guard.

She no more thought of lying than she had of running. "I have dreamed that underneath this bridge there is a treasure, and I have traveled a long way to find that treasure and be rich," she said.

"That's strange," said the guard. "Just last night I too had a dream. I dreamed that in the city of Krakow, on the street of the Lost Sheep, in a basement flat on the corner, there lies a treasure buried behind the wardrobe. But it was only a dream; it can never be true. Now, you, you get out of here before I run you in. And don't come back!"

She hurried away and began the long journey back to Krakow. Arriving there, she went straight to her apartment in the street of the Lost Sheep, moved the wardrobe, dug into the wall behind it and found the treasure, sufficient to keep her and her children for the rest of their lives.

The treasure had, of course, been with the widow all her poverty-stricken life. She only found it as the result of faith in her dream, and a long journey. The guard might have discovered the same treasure, but he had no time for visions. Godzone is equally close to home and as often missed. Donkeyfaced pragmatists analyze the world into fragments, and miss its Maker. They build their fine sieves of steel wire and disregard moonbeams because they can't be caught. They know all about method and nothing about mystery. They guard the bridges and dismiss their dreams, and so trade their inheritance for a mass of pedantry.

Homecoming

You, however, have the hunger for God in your heart and the itch of the road in your feet. What your eyes have already been opened to will haunt you now like the scent of a childhood memory.

Godzone is yours to explore, from here to the edge of the world. And beyond the world, when the compromises and midnight aches loose their long-fingered grip, God waits to welcome you home.

The Zone is your natural habitat. It is what you were created for. Unused talents and frustrated desires may seem as useless to you now as fingers to the fetal Chopin. The time will come when all will make sense. The black hole in your heart has begun to be invaded by God. In the fullness of the Zone, God will be with you in such a way that you will not know where you stop and God starts. Like two old and tender lovers folding their bodies so perfectly together, there will be consummation of the deep tide of love that sucks and worries at the currents of your heart. You will be whole and healed and held.

Only wanderers like us know the discomfort of being so far from the place where we belong. Who can describe the way we know ourselves and what we mean, and the muddled hints that are all we can convey to other people? How do you describe the sheer joy of being alive, which never quite empties the vaults of remorse; the longing for something that only grows stronger when goals are achieved; the strength of goodwill and the weakness of efforts to enact it; the love for those we leave behind and the inability to stay with them; the hunger to hear our own language spoken, and by a voice we know? This land between the ages is not our homeland, and we can never settle here. We must move on, pressing towards the end of the road, which never seems to end. Its end, of course, is God. We ragged refugees have a home, and we will come to it. The crowds of unseen onlookers will cheer us across that last stretch; our brother Jesus take us by the hand and lead us in. There you will find such a collection of geeks and oddballs and misfits as you never thought possible, and you will be at home with them—and in them and through them and around them, God. Oh, and in the distance, something awfully familiar. The road. What did you expect? Clouds and harps maybe?

Back to the Road

For the present, the journey continues. Back on this side of the river, there is distance to cover and people to meet. There is the truck driver who pops speed to stay awake, and every now and again provides excitement by swerving his twenty-eight-ton rig to avoid the gnomes he sees. There is the straight-laced and ancient granny who puts a tablecloth over the roadside picnic table and slips money into your hand as you retrieve your pack from her trunk. There is the ruddy farmer whose front seat you share with his dog, which you remember by the fleas that are still biting a week later. There is the neurotic insurance agent who relates the whole of her sorry love-life, emphasizing points by looking deeply and moistly into your eyes and terrorizing oncoming traffic.

There are adventures to be had. Perhaps you have not yet met the friendly guide who will relieve you of your passport, your travelers checks, and your faith in human nature; slept on the top of a moving truck under the desert stars of Africa; woken to the feel of a rough and passionate lick from a cow with its head through the flap of your tent; cried with the fire of a "mild" Indian curry; argued with a hundred pompous border officials with a hundred different reasons why your visa is not valid; shared your life story with someone who doesn't understand a word you say; evacuated your innards over a hole in the floor until you imagine your brain will follow them.

At times Godzone will seem a romantic dream. You will think yourself gullible to have entertained its existence. You will crack cynical jokes about dreamers and dimwits. You will hurt yourself and others to prove how cool and clever and tough you really are. This book you will lay aside and forget. Insights that once gripped you will fade until you doubt they taught you anything. The day may come when you will discard visions of a Zone beyond the world as impossible and immature. Does Godzone exist? Is it nothing more than a utopian stirring in the heart of a humanity that will not accept its mortality?

Once there was a very wise old man whose advice was sought from all corners of the kingdom. A young and jealous prince set out to humble the old man.

"I will go to the sage with a bird in my hand and ask him if it is alive or dead," he decided. "If he says it is alive, I will crush the bird in my hand and kill it. If he says that it is dead,

I will open my hand and let it fly away." The smug prince traveled many days and eventually arrived at the old man's humble house. "Tell me, old man, is this bird alive or dead?" he asked.

The stooped prophet looked deep into the man's eyes, and said quietly, "The answer lies in your hand."

SOURCES

The stories in this book are adapted from or inspired by many different sources. The following have been especially helpful, and thanks are due to their publishers:

Storytelling: Imagination and Faith by William J. Bausch (Twenty-Third Publications, 1984).

The Song of the Bird by Anthony De Mello (Gujarat Sahitya Prakash, 1987).

Jerusalem Daybook by James K. Baxter (Price Milburn, 1971).

Grasshopper on the Road by Arnold Lobel (HarperCollins, 1986).